BASS!

Proven Strategies, Skills & Secrets for Catching

More and Bigger Largemouth Bass

SHADY OAK PRESS

BASS!

Proven Strategies, Skills & Secrets for Catching More and Bigger Largemouth Bass

Tom Carpenter
Creative Director

Jen Weaverling
Production Editor

Jenya Prosmitsky, Kate Opseth
Book Design & Production

Gina Germ
Photo Editor

Randy Hoepner
Front Cover Design

Photography
Principal Photography by Bill Lindner Photography (Bill Lindner, Tom Heck, Mike Hehner, Pete Cozad, Jason Lund)

Additional Photography
Denver Bryan, pp. 42
Mark Emery, pp. 26, 28, 29, 31, 33, 34, 35 all, 41, 136–137
Tom Evans, p. 51 all
©Zig Leszczynski/Animals, Animals, p. 132(2)
©Ted Levin/Animals, Animals, p. 131
Larry Mishkar, pp. 8, 26(2), 43
Steve Pennaz, pp. 76, 151
Roger Peterson, pp. 26, 41
Doug Stamm, pp. 29(2), 30, 33, 37, 49(3), 50
Dick Sternberg, pp. 31(2), 37, 41(2), 44(2), 45, 47(3), 66(2), 73, 133

Illustration
David Rottinghaus, pp. 16 all, 17 all, 111
David Schelitzche, pp. 66, 80-81, 92, 131, 132(2), 147
Joe Tommelleri, pp. 10, 11 all

1 2 3 4 5 6 / 12 11 10 09 08 07
©1999 North American Membership Group, Inc.
ISBN: 978-1-58159-318-1

Distributed by:
Sterling Publishing Co., Inc.
387 Park Avenue South
New York, NY 10016-8810

For information about custom editions, special sales, premium and corporate purchases, please contact Sterling Special Sales Department at 800-805-5489 or specialsales@sterlingpub.com.

The Author
Dick Sternberg's broad-spectrum knowledge of bass fishing is easy to recognize in this complete guide to catching North America's favorite gamefish.

SHADY OAK PRESS

12301 Whitewater Drive
Minnetonka, MN 55343

CONTENTS

INTRODUCTION

Largemouth bass offer everything you could ask for in a fish. They're available—found coast-to-coast. They get big—from five-pounders up north to ten-pounds-plus down south and out west. They fight—who doesn't thrill to the spectacular leaps and bull-dogging runs of an energetic largemouth? And they offer variety.

Here's what variety means. Bass are found in all types of waters—the farm pond down the road, massive man-made reservoirs, natural lakes that are small or sprawling, big or medium-sized rivers and small to tiny creeks, coastal rivers and brackish backwaters, and more. What's more, largemouths eat a wide variety of forage items, and you can catch them on a variety of baits and lures.

But all this variety adds up to challenge: Largemouth bass can be hard to find and catch. Understanding and knowledge are the most important tools you can put to work on the water to solve the bass fishing puzzles that face all serious anglers.

Catching more and bigger bass comes down to knowing the fish, figuring out where they will be today, and finding the right presentation to get them to hit.

BASS! will make you an all-around better bass angler. This book looks in-depth at the biology of this fascinating fish, helps you understand where bass live and what they eat, then outlines step-by-step the strategies, techniques, tackle and lures you need to find consistent bass-fishing success.

You'll find a lot of enjoyment and reward on the journey. But it all starts here. Enjoy *BASS!* And catch more of them.

THE FISH

*B*ecoming a competent bass angler starts with a thorough understanding of your quarry.

UNDERSTANDING LARGEMOUTH BASS

More than 10 million American anglers are in love with the largemouth bass. For many people, bass fishing is a passion that consumes practically all of their leisure time. They own an expensive bass boat completely rigged with state-of-the-art electronics, a dozen expensive rods and reels, and several tackle boxes stuffed with every imaginable bass lure. Even when they can't go fishing, they're probably watching someone haul in bass on TV.

So why this tremendous interest in largemouth fishing? Here are some likely explanations:

• Largemouth are the most widely distributed gamefish in North America. They are found in all the lower 48 states and their range extends into southern Canada, Mexico and Cuba. As a result, practically every American angler can find largemouth within a short drive of his or her home.

• The largemouth's diet includes practically any kind of living organism that will fit into its mouth. This makes largemouth quite "angler-friendly," meaning that they will strike practically any kind of artificial lure or live bait and will feed on the bottom, on the surface or anywhere in between.

• Largemouth are powerful fighters. Although they're not as acrobatic as smallmouth, they don't hesitate to take to the air to throw a lure. If your tackle is too light, they'll wrap you around weeds or brush, quickly ending the battle.

To improve your angling success, it pays to become a student of largemouth behavior. The pages that follow will give you some insight into the habits and "personality" of this amazing freshwater predator.

A cartwheeling largemouth tests the skill of even the most experienced angler.

LARGEMOUTH BASICS

Largemouth bass belong to the sunfish family but, more specifically, they are members of a group of fishes called "black bass." Besides largemouth, the group includes all other members of the genus *Micropterus*, namely smallmouth, spotted, redeye, Suwannee and Guadalupe bass. Largemouth are the biggest, the most widespread and certainly the most popular of the black bass clan.

The largemouth is aptly named; its mouth is noticeably larger than that of any of its close relatives, explaining why so many anglers refer to it as *bigmouth* or *bucketmouth*.

Taxonomists recognize two subspecies of largemouth bass: the northern largemouth (*Micropterus salmoides salmoides*) and the Florida largemouth (*Micropterus salmoides floridanus*). The two subspecies look nearly identical, but Florida bass have slightly smaller scales. Originally found only in the Florida Peninsula, Florida bass have been stocked in several other southern states, most notably California and Texas.

Florida bass grow considerably faster than northern largemouth, generally reaching a weight of 10 pounds in only 8 years; and there are several 20-plus pounders on record. A northern largemouth would typically weigh about 5 pounds at that age. Attempts have been made to stock Florida bass in the North, but in the coldwater environment they grow no faster than northern bass.

The world-record largemouth, a 22-pound, 4-ouncer caught in Montgomery Lake, Georgia, in 1932, may have been an "intergrade," a cross between a Florida and northern largemouth.

The life span of a largemouth seldom exceeds 10 years, although they have been known to live as long as 16 in the northern part of their range.

Largemouth bass are greenish to tannish in color with a darker back, lighter belly and a dark horizontal band. The jaw is longer than that of the smallmouth, extending past the rear of the eye.

Largemouth bass range.

The Largemouth's Close Relatives

Smallmouth bass are greenish to bronze in color, accounting for their common name, "bronzeback." They have dark vertical bars or diamond patterns on the side, but these marks are not always present and may come and go. The cheek also has dark bars. The jaw extends to approximately the middle of the eye, which is often reddish.

Spotted bass have light greenish sides with a dark lateral band consisting of irregular blotches. The jaw is shorter than that of a largemouth, but longer than that of a smallmouth, extending nearly to the rear of the eye. Each scale below the lateral band may have a distinct dark spot. Spotted bass have a small patch of teeth on their tongue.

Redeye bass get their name from the distinctive reddish eye. The sides and back are brownish with darker blotches. The gill cover has a large black spot and the jaw extends nearly to the rear of the eye. Some redeyes have reddish rear fins, blue spots on the back and sides, and a bluish belly.

Suwannee bass are the smallest black bass, seldom exceeding 12 inches in length. The cheeks, breast and belly are bright turquoise. There are a series of dark vertical blotches along the lateral line and a distinct black spot at the base of the tail. The jaw extends to the rear of the eye.

Guadalupe bass are generally greenish and have a lateral band consisting of separate dark blotches. They resemble spotted bass in that the scales below the lateral line are spotted, but the greenish coloration extends much lower on the body. The jaw extends to the rear of the eye.

The flash and vibration from the blade of a spinnerbait draws the attention of bass from a distance.

Largemouth Senses

Largemouth bass rely on the same five senses as most other predator fish, using different senses to varying degrees depending upon the environment in which they live.

• **Vision.** Most authorities agree that largemouth rely primarily on vision to find food and escape predators. Their large eyes are located on the upper sides of their head, so they can see well in all directions, except straight back and straight down. How far they can see depends mainly on water clarity. In very clear water, they likely can see more than 30 feet.

Every serious bass angler knows that the fish can recognize color. Practically every old bass lure you see has at least a touch of red on it, and for good reason. Laboratory tests have shown that red is the color largemouth recognize most readily. But that doesn't necessarily mean you should always use red lures.

Water filters out color and red is the first color to disappear, usually at a depth of about 10 feet. At that point, the color is distinguishable only as a shade of gray. As a rule, bright or fluorescent colors work best in discolored water; dark or drab colors in clear water. But the only sure way to determine the best color is to experiment.

• **Lateral Line.** The lateral line consists of a row of pores along each side of the fish, extending from the gill to the base of the tail. The pores are connected to a network of nerve endings that sense the slightest vibrations and transmit them to receptors in the inner ear.

The lateral-line sense enables bass to pick up vibrations in the water that help them determine not only if predators or prey are present, but how big they are, how fast they're moving and in what direction.

In clear water, bass use their lateral-line sense to detect prey at a distance and then swim close enough that they can use their vision to make an accurate strike. But in low-clarity water they often rely entirely on their lateral-line sense. In one experiment, researchers covered the eyes of bass and then released them into a tank, along with some minnows. Even with their eyes covered, the bass were able to locate and eat the minnows.

• **Hearing.** Bass lack external ears, but they have inner ears consisting of tiny bones that pick up even subtle sounds, like the clicking noise produced by a crayfish.

This explains why many anglers use lures with rattles, especially when fishing at night or in low-clarity water.

• **Smell & Taste.** Compared to scent-oriented species such as catfish, largemouth bass have a poorly developed sense of smell. Although there is no precise method for measuring their ability to detect odors, the number of olfactory folds in their nasal chamber provides a good indication. Whereas catfish have about 140 folds, largemouth generally have less than 20, meaning that they have considerably fewer scent receptors.

Except in the murkiest water, it is unlikely that bass rely heavily on their sense of smell to find food or avoid predators. Nevertheless, many fishermen believe that scented lures improve their success, mainly because bass seem to hold onto them a lit-

tle longer, giving the angler extra time to set the hook.

Taste is also relatively unimportant in largemouth feeding activity. But some anglers believe that salted worms and other flavored baits dramatically increase their catch rate.

Appealing to the Largemouth's Senses

Gaudy colors such as bright orange, hot pink, brilliant chartreuse and electric green represent nothing a bass encounters in nature, but they often trigger more strikes than natural-colored lures.

Lures that create sound or vibration are often more effective than those that do not. Many experienced bass anglers swear by rattlebaits, bladebaits and noisy topwaters.

Food Habits

Soon after hatching, a largemouth bass begins feeding on tiny aquatic animals called *zooplankton.* As the fish increase in size, they focus on larger food items, primarily insects. By the end of their first summer, when they reach a length of 4 to 7 inches, they're feeding mainly on small fish.

Although fish are usually the most important food source for the remainder of their adult life, largemouth will take most any kind of food that will fit into their mouth. They commonly eat crayfish, mice, salamanders, frogs, worms, leeches, snails, turtles and even small snakes.

As a rule, largemouth will take bigger food items than smallmouth, probably because their mouth is so much larger. It's not unusual, for example, for a largemouth to grab a baitfish half its own length. This explains why fishermen do not hesitate to use foot-long baitfish to catch trophy bass.

Largemouth take big food items much differently than small ones. Small morsels are literally "inhaled"; the bass darts to within inches of its prey, flares its gills and sucks in a volume of water containing its food. The excess water and any other debris is then expelled through the gill openings.

If the food item won't fit easily into its mouth, the bass grabs it any way it can: head-first, sideways or even by the tail. But it always turns the prey in order to swallow it headfirst; otherwise, the spiny dorsal fin of a large baitfish would catch in the bass's throat.

Largemouth feed most heavily at water temperatures from the upper 60s to about 80°F. Feeding slows considerably at water temperatures above 85 or below 50, although anglers in the North catch a few largemouth through the ice.

With a mouth like this, a big bass can easily swallow a foot-long baitfish.

A largemouth often grabs its prey sideways or even by the tail. Then it will gradually turn the prey to the headfirst position by alternately loosening its grip and then biting down again.

After working the prey into the headfirst position, the bass momentarily releases it and then immediately swallows it.

If the baitfish is too large to swallow completely, the bass will swallow as much as it can, leaving the tail protruding from its mouth and gradually digesting the rest of its body. The digestion process may take 2 or 3 days.

Ambush Feeding. *During periods of food abundance, largemouth often lie motionless in dense weedy or woody cover, or in the shade of a rock or log, waiting for unsuspecting prey to come too close. Then, with a sudden burst of speed, they grab the prey and return to their resting spot.*

Cruising. *When food is scarce, hungry bass must cruise about to find a meal rather than wait for food to come to them. Although it is difficult for a single bass to get within striking distance of baitfish, it may encounter an injured minnow, a crayfish, a leech or some other slow-moving food item.*

Feeding in Loose Schools. *Largemouth commonly comb the shallows in loose schools, looking for food. When a baitfish sees an approaching bass, it darts away, often right into the path of another bass. This feeding method enables largemouth to capture baitfish that would otherwise easily escape.*

Open-Water Pack Feeding. *When bass are feeding on open-water baitfish, such as shad, they often feed in much the same manner as white bass or stripers. The pack surrounds a school of baitfish, driving them to the surface and slashing at them from below. At times, you'll see bass boiling on the surface.*

A fast-growing bass has a small head compared to the rest of its body.

Growth

The growth rate of the largemouth bass varies tremendously throughout its range. In some waters, the fish reach a length of 14 inches and a weight of nearly 2 pounds by the end of their first year. In other waters, the fish attain a length of only 2 inches and a weight of a fraction of an ounce in the same amount of time.

These great differences in growth rate are a result of the following:

• **Length of Growing Season.** The water temperature in which largemouth can grow (50° to 80°F) persists for only about 5 months in the extreme northern part of their range; in the southern part, it lasts at least twice that long. So it's not surprising that southern bass often weigh twice as much as northern bass of the same age.

But that doesn't necessarily mean that southern largemouth always reach a larger size, because northern bass generally live longer. The maximum life span of a northern bass is about 16 years, compared to only about 10 years for a southern bass.

The longer life span explains why the average size of tournament-caught bass is often larger in the North than in the South.

• **Genetics.** Of course, the average Florida bass grows considerably faster than the average northern largemouth (chart, opposite). But there also may be noticeable differences in growth rate even among the same subspecies.

As most veteran bass anglers know, certain waters routinely produce big largemouth while others in the same region rarely do. In many cases, the difference can be attributed to genetics.

• **Water Fertility.** Largemouth generally grow fastest in waters of high fertility, because they offer more food than infertile waters.

Highly fertile waters have an abundance of plankton, the basic link in the aquatic food chain. As a rule, the more plankton, the more baitfish.

• **Predator-Prey Balance.** Bass grow most rapidly in situations where there are a relatively small number of predators competing for the available forage. Where largemouth are super-

Growth Rates of Largemouth Bass from North to South

(Northern Subspecies)

Location	Length (Inches) at End of Each Year								
	1	2	3	4	5	6	7	8	9
Three Fork Ponds, Montana	1.9	3.8	5.7	7.7	9.9	11.5	12.9	13.8	14.7
Clear Lake, Iowa	4.1	9.5	12.9	14.8	16.0	17.0	17.9	18.9	—
Lake of the Ozarks, Missouri	5.3	8.2	11.2	13.2	14.3	16.6	18.5	19.7	20.0
Center Hill Lake, Tennessee	5.0	10.0	17.0	18.0	19.0	20.5	21.0	21.5	22.0

abundant or where there are large numbers of competing gamefish, such as walleyes or striped bass, growth is considerably slower.

• **Male vs. Female.** Although male and female largemouth grow at approximately the same rate in most waters, females usually live longer than males. As a result, the vast majority of trophy bass are females.

Growth Rate of Northern vs. Florida Largemouth

(In El Capitan Reservoir, California)

NORTHERN LARGEMOUTH			FLORIDA LARGEMOUTH		
Age	Length (Inches)	Weight (Pounds)	Age	Length (Inches)	Weight (Pounds)
1	6.1	0.2	1	5.9	0.2
2	11.6	1.1	2	12.8	1.5
3	14.7	2.2	3	15.7	2.8
4	16.4	2.9	4	17.7	4.2
5	17.9	3.8	5	20.4	6.4
6	19.1	4.6	6	22.1	8.3
7	20.3	5.4	7	23.1	9.6
8	20.4	5.5	8	23.4	10.1
9	—	—	9	24.8	12.2
10	—	—	10	25.6	13.3

Spawning Habits

Spawning activity of largemouth bass can be broken into three distinct stages. Where you find the fish and how they behave depends on what stage of the spawn they are in.

• **Pre-Spawn.** When water temperatures rise into the upper 40s, largemouth begin moving out of their deep winter haunts. They congregate on shallow flats that are easily warmed by the sun. In natural lakes, they move into shallow, weedy bays, boat channels and harbors (pp. 36-41). In man-made lakes, they're drawn to shallow flats adjacent to old river channels or to creek channels, brushy upper ends of creek arms and wooded coves (pp. 29-35). In big rivers, you'll find them in weedy sloughs, side channels and stump fields (pp. 48-49).

Because of their developing gonads, the fish require more energy than normal, so they are feeding heavily. But they're very susceptible to cold fronts, which drive them back to deeper water and slow or stop their feeding activity.

• **Spawn.** Spawning is triggered by a combination of water temperature and day length. Male largemouth begin fanning out nests in the shallows when the water temperature rises into the 60s and stays there for a few days.

A period of very warm weather in early spring may quickly bring the water temperature in the shallows up to the 60s. But that doesn't necessarily mean that largemouth will start to spawn. Their biological clock, which is controlled by day length, tells them that the time is not yet right. Warmer than usual water temperatures may move spawning ahead by a few days, but seldom more than that.

If spawning were regulated by water temperature alone, there could be grave biological consequences. In an early spring, the fry would hatch much earlier than normal, making them that much more vulnerable to an early spring cold front that could wipe out the supply of plankton that the fry need for food. The result would be mass starvation that would wipe out

It's not unusual for a spawning male to be considerably smaller than the female.

much of the year class.

Largemouth normally nest in an area that is sheltered from the wind, usually around weedy or woody cover. Using his tail, the male fans away silt to reach a firm sandy or gravelly bottom. Then the female moves in to deposit her eggs.

The fish generally build their nests in the vicinity of their pre-spawn locations, usually moving a little shallower to find a suitable bottom or some type of cover. In natural lakes, you'll often find spawning beds on sand-gravel areas along an otherwise muddy shoreline or around old patches of lily pads, maidencane or bulrushes from the previous year.

In man-made lakes, the fish

Approximate Spawning Times of Largemouth Bass

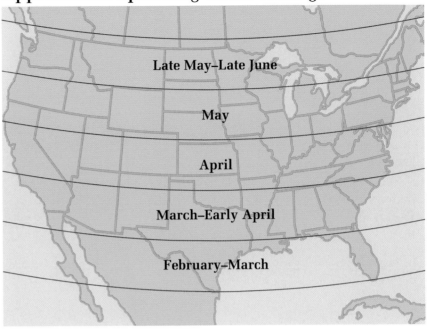

Late May–Late June

May

April

March–Early April

February–March

usually nest in or on tree roots, around brush piles or in some other type of woody cover.

In big rivers, most spawning takes place in weedy backwaters, but the fish may also spawn in woody cover in side channels with light current.

By the time the water temperature reaches the upper 60s, most spawning has been completed. The male guards the nest and remains with the fry until they disperse.

• **Post-Spawn.** Female largemouth are notoriously difficult to catch following completion of spawning. Not only are they feeding sporadically as they recuperate from the rigors of spawning, they may be hard to find as they make their way from their spawning sites to the deeper structure where they will spend the summer.

Males, however, are easy to catch as long as they are guarding the nest. They too are feeding only sporadically,

but they will attack anything that comes too close to the nest, including an angler's lure. But catching nest-guarding males is frowned upon by most of the bass-fishing community. Once the male is removed, sunfish and other panfish can easily raid the nest, quickly eating most of the defenseless fry.

• **Duration of Spawning Period.** In the northern part of the largemouth's range, the entire spawning period (pre-spawn through post-spawn) lasts only 2 or 3 weeks. Because the water warms so rapidly, spawning activity is compressed into a much shorter period than it is in the southern part of the range.

In Florida, for example, some fish may start to spawn in January while others may not begin until late March. Consequently, anglers can find bass on the spawning beds for a period of two or even three months, depending on how fast the water warms.

THE WATERS

If you don't know where to find the bass, you can't catch them—even with the most expensive equipment and the best lures.

LARGEMOUTH HABITAT

Largemouth bass have the uncanny ability to survive in almost any kind of warmwater environment. You'll find them in shallow, weed-choked natural lakes, deep reservoirs with practically no weeds, small creeks, big rivers, golf-course ponds and any other kind of depression in the ground that can permanently hold water.

But even though large-mouth are one of the most adaptable freshwater game-fish, there are limits as to what they can tolerate. Following are their habitat needs and preferences.

Water Temperature

Like all members of the sunfish family, largemouth are classified as warmwater fish. Their preferred tempera-ture range is 68° to 78°F, but they can tolerate water tem-peratures as high as the low 90s. They can survive near-freezing temperatures in win-ter but, given a choice, will seek out areas where the water is warmer. This explains why they congregate in deep holes in natural lakes and why they're often found around heated discharges from power plants.

Florida largemouth are much less tolerant of cold water than northern largemouth. When Florida bass were stocked in northern lakes, many did not survive the winter. Temperature-tolerance studies conducted on Florida bass show that water temperatures in the mid-40s can be lethal.

As discussed earlier, feeding activity of largemouth slows considerably at water temperatures above 85°F and below 50 (p. 14).

Dissolved Oxygen

Largemouth bass require fairly high levels of dissolved oxygen. When held in water of 77°F, bass showed signs of stress, such as rapid gill movements, at an oxygen level of 5 parts per million (ppm), which is adequate for many kinds of gamefish. Signs of stress abated at 6 ppm.

Other experiments determined that bass grow most rapidly when dissolved oxygen is near saturation levels (about 9 ppm at 70°F and 8 ppm at 80).

Their high oxygen requirement is one important reason why largemouth are generally found in shallow water. The upper layer of a lake contains the most oxygen, because the water is constantly circulated by the wind.

The oxygen needs of largemouth are also evident in *winterkill* lakes, those that experience very low oxygen levels in late winter. As oxygen levels decline, largemouth are one of the first fish to show signs of stress and they are among the first to die when oxygen levels drop too low.

Largemouth favor shallow, weedy water not only because it is rich in food and cover, but because it generally has a high level of dissolved oxygen.

Cover

Few other freshwater fish are as cover-oriented as the largemouth bass. From the moment they hatch, bass fry take cover under lily pads and other floating vegetation to minimize the threat of attack from predatory birds. After leaving the nest, they move into dense submergent weeds where they can hide from predatory fish.

In most cases, adult bass do not require cover for protection from predators, but they use it for shade, shelter from current and as an ambush point. Adult bass utilize a wide variety of cover including rocks, logs, flooded timber and brush, as well as submergent, emergent and floating-leaved vegetation.

Cover may also serve merely as a reference point, something different in their surroundings to which they can relate. Researchers found that bass placed in a plain white tank tended to congregate around a black stripe painted on the side.

Bottom Type

Largemouth can be found over a variety of bottom types, depending mainly on their food source. In early spring, for example, they commonly move into mud-bottomed bays because these bays warm earlier than other parts of the lake and are the first to attract baitfish.

In summer, you'll often find largemouth around rock piles that hold crayfish, which rank high on their list of favorite foods.

Important Types of Largemouth Cover

Hiding Cover. *Juvenile largemouth rely on weedy or brushy cover as protection from predators such as fish-eating birds and larger gamefish.*

Current Break. *Stream-dwelling largemouth use boulders, logjams and other objects to provide shelter from the current.*

Ambush Cover. *Broad-leaved weeds, submerged timber and other dense cover conceal bass from unsuspecting prey.*

Shade. *Floating-leaved plants, fallen trees and even steep cliff faces provide shade and slightly cooler water temperatures.*

Although largemouth may be found almost anywhere along a weedline, they normally focus on the hard-bottomed portions. That's because a hard bottom generally produces more invertebrate life than a soft one. Baitfish congregate over the hard bottom to pick off the invertebrates. The bass, in turn, pick off the baitfish. This also explains why a patch of hard bottom in an otherwise soft basin can be a largemouth magnet.

Salt Tolerance

Largemouth are more salt-tolerant than most freshwater fish, which explains why they are commonly found in tidewater rivers. Studies have shown that largemouth bass can withstand a salinity as high as 24.4 parts per thousand (ppt), considerably higher than any other kind of black bass. Spotted bass, for example, were able to tolerate a salinity of only 11.8 ppt and were seldom found in waters with a salinity above 3.5 ppt.

A gravel patch or rock pile on an otherwise soft bottom will almost surely attract largemouth.

Acidity

The acidity (or alkalinity) of water is measured in pH units. A pH of 7 is neutral; below 7, acidic; and above 7, alkaline. Largemouth can tolerate a broad pH range, from about 6.1 to 9.5. Practically all bass waters fall within that range. Largemouth can also tolerate rapid changes in pH level.

Despite this fact, pH is often billed as a very important factor in determining largemouth location and behavior. Some anglers even buy pH meters and use them to find water with the "ideal" pH.

Even if PH has some minimal effect on largemouth location and behavior, other factors such as food availability, temperature and oxygen level would certainly override it.

Clarity

You can find largemouth in Florida springs with some of the clearest water in the world, but they can also survive in turbid rivers where you lose sight of your lure an inch beneath the surface.

Although clarity has little effect on their ability to survive, it does affect their growth rate. Studies have consistently shown that largemouth grow faster in clear waters, probably because they can easily feed by sight, the most effective method.

Largemouth thrive in ultraclear water, such as this Florida spring.

MAN-MADE LAKES

Whether you call them reservoirs, impoundments, artificial lakes or man-made lakes, this diverse category of waters probably produces more largemouth bass than all other water types combined.

Man-made lakes differ from natural lakes in many important respects.

• Water levels fluctuate dramatically because of runoff, power generation, flood control and irrigation.

• The fluctuating water limits weed growth; the major cover is more likely to be flooded timber and brush, or man-made objects such as flooded house foundations.

• Because man-made lakes are created by damming a river or stream, the basins tend to be long and narrow, with the greatest depth toward the downstream end.

• Silt carried in by the river reduces clarity in the upstream end of the lake; the water gradually clears toward the downstream end.

• With the constant inflow of water, man-made lakes seldom have low oxygen levels, even in winter.

Largemouth bass are found in man-made lakes of practically all classes. Here's where to find the fish in each important type:

Swampland Reservoirs

These lakes were created by damming a stream running through low-lying, swampy terrain. In most such lakes, the bottom is relatively flat and there are few distinct creek arms. There is an abundance of flooded timber, the water is highly fertile and often has a tannic stain, and the maximum depth is 50 feet.

Besides largemouth, these lakes often produce crappies, sunfish and catfish, white bass and chain pickerel in addition to carp, gar and other roughfish.

Largemouth Bass Locations in Swampland Reservoirs During ...

Pre-Spawn
• Shallow flats adjacent to old river channels or creek channels.
• Shallow flats along shoreline.
• Shallow lips around islands.

Spawn
• Weedy shoreline flats.
• In dense, shallow cypress thickets.
• On top of shallow cypress roots.

Shallow, weedy flats along the shoreline make good spawning areas.

Post-Spawn through Early Fall
• Deep cypress flats.
• Deep bays.
• Deep sloughs (areas that held water before the lake filled).
• Edges of old river channel.
• Main-lake points.

Late Fall and Winter
• Confluence of slough and main river channel.
• Deepest areas of old river channel.
• Deep creek channels.

Dense, shallow cypress thickets draw spawning bass.

Look for late-season bass at the confluence of a slough and the main river channel.

Flatland Reservoirs

Flatland Reservoirs differ from swampland reservoirs in that they are located on higher terrain, their basins are considerably deeper and they have distinct (although short) creek arms. Even though the maximum depth may be 100 feet or more, most of the water is in the 30- to 60-foot range and the bottom is relatively flat.

Most lakes of this type are surrounded by agricultural land, so water fertility is high and plankton is abundant. As a result, these lakes produce tremendous crops of shad and other baitfish.

Although flooded timber and brush furnishes good cover for largemouth bass, many of these lakes have a fair amount of weed growth. The water levels do not fluc-

tuate as much as in most other types of man-made lakes, so the plants can take root.

In addition to largemouth, most of these lakes have good populations of sunfish, crappies, white bass and catfish, and many have been stocked with striped bass or "wipers" (striped bass/white bass hybrids).

Largemouth Bass Locations in Flatland Reservoirs During ...

Pre-Spawn/Spawn
- Brushy upper ends of creek arms.
- Wooded coves.
- Timbered flats adjacent to upper ends of creek channels.

Post-Spawn through Mid-Fall
- Timbered flats along main river channel and deeper creek channels.
- Humps near river and creek channels.
- Flooded fencerows.
- Flooded roadbeds and road ditches.
- Flooded ponds and stock tanks.
- Timbered main-lake points.

Late Fall and Winter
- Deep holes in creek.

Brushy flats at the upper end of creek arms are the primary spawning areas.

Bass also spawn in wooded coves, either in creek arms or the main lake.

Bass often feed on timbered humps near the main river channel. After feeding, they can easily retreat to deep water in the channel.

Flooded roadbeds make good summertime feeding areas; the ditches alongside them, resting areas.

Hill-land/Highland Reservoirs

As their names suggest, these reservoirs are found in hilly or mountainous country. The main lake is generally long and narrow with relatively long creek arms. The maximum depth is usually more than 100 feet and the shoreline slopes quite rapidly.

With water fertility low to moderate in most of these lakes, the water is relatively clear. In spring, however, heavy runoff often discolors the upper end of the lake.

Because most of these reservoirs were created for purposes of flood control or power generation, the water level fluctuates tremendously

(often 50 feet or more) over the course of the year. This greatly limits growth of rooted aquatic plants. Gamefish usually rely on woody or rocky cover.

The predominant types of gamefish often include largemouth and smallmouth bass, white and striped bass, crappies and sunfish. A few reser-

Largemouth Bass Locations in Hill-land/Highland Reservoirs During ...

Pre-Spawn/Spawn
- Brushy upper ends of main creek arms.
- Brushy secondary and tertiary creek arms.
- Brushy coves off the main lake.
- Shale banks.

Post-Spawn through Mid-Fall
- Major points in creek arms.
- Rocky main-lake points.
- Main-lake points with timbered lips.
- Suspended off bluff faces.
- Edges of creek channels and main river channel, particularly along outside bends.

Late Fall and Winter
- Suspended over deep water in creek channels and main river channel.
- Suspended off main-lake points.
- Junctions of main river channel and creek channels.
- Discolored water in upper ends of creek arms after heavy rain.

Brushy flats at the upper end of a creek arm make a prime spawning area for largemouth.

Outside bends along creek channels and the main river channel hold good numbers of largemouth in summer, especially if there is timber along the upper lip of the slope.

After a heavy late-season rain, bass move into the muddy water at the upper ends of creek arms.

voirs have been stocked with muskies or walleyes, and some of the deeper ones hold rainbow or brown trout. Shad are usually the most plentiful forage fish, although skipjack herring abound in some of these lakes.

After the spawn through mid-fall, bass will suspend off bluff faces.

Canyon Reservoirs

Located in narrow gorges in mountainous terrain, primarily in the western states, canyon reservoirs are the deepest type of man-made lake. The maximum depth is usually several hundred feet. Because they are fed mainly by snowmelt, the water is cold, clear and infertile. The main lake is long and narrow, as are the creek arms. In fact, the two may be difficult to distinguish.

Most canyon reservoirs were constructed to supply water for power generation, but some are also used for purposes of irrigation and flood control. The water level on most of these lakes remains fairly stable throughout the year, but flood-control reservoirs may fluctuate as much as 100 feet.

Because of the infertile water and steep banks, weed growth is minimal. Bass find some cover along rocky cliff walls and what little timber remains on points and in the back ends of creek arms. The low fertility also limits food production, so bass grow slowly and seldom reach trophy size.

Although most canyon reservoirs are better suited for trout than bass, many have surprisingly good largemouth populations. Some are also managed for smallmouth bass, striped bass and wipers.

Largemouth Bass Locations in Canyon Reservoirs During ...

Pre-Spawn
- Points at junction of main lake and spawning cove.
- Steep bluffs leading into back ends of coves.

Spawn
- Sand-gravel ledges at upper ends of coves.

Post-Spawn through Mid-Fall
- Gradually tapering broken-rock points in creek arms and main lake.
- Shaded cuts along cliff walls.
- Rock slides along cliff walls.
- Extended lips along cliff walls, especially those with a rubble bottom.

- Cliff faces.

Late Fall and Winter
- Steep-sloping stair-step areas along cliff walls.
- Sharp-sloping points in creek arms and main lake.

Points just outside spawning coves concentrate largemouth prior to spawning.

Shallow sand-gravel ledges in spawning coves, especially those with brushy cover, draw spawning largemouth.

Broken-rock points and humps with a slow taper hold bass from late spring well into the fall.

During the cold-weather months, bass congregate along cliff walls, especially near steep-sloping, stair-step areas.

NATURAL LAKES

Largemouth bass inhabit a wide variety of natural lakes ranging from the deep "shield" lakes of Canada to knee-deep marshes in Florida. As a rule, warm, shallow lakes with heavy weed growth produce more bass than deep, cold lakes with little vegetation. But even frigid northern lakes often have warm, shallow, weedy bays that are good bass producers.

On the pages that follow are the types of natural lakes that are best suited for largemouth bass. For each of these lake types, we'll show you where to catch bass during each season.

Northern Eutrophic Lakes

These lakes have warm, shallow, fertile water of low to medium clarity. Weed growth (including stands of emergent, submergent or floating-leaved weeds) is heavy and may extend into the middle of the lake. The bottom consists primarily of mud or silt, with scattered patches of sand, gravel or rock. Most of these lakes develop a distinct thermocline in summer.

Largemouth Bass Locations in Northern Eutrophic Lakes During ...

Pre-Spawn
- Shallow bays that warm earlier than the main lake.
- Boat channels and harbors.
- New growths of submergent weeds, like cabbage or coontail.

Spawn
- Old patches of lily pads or bulrushes from the previous year.
- Sand-gravel areas along an otherwise muddy shoreline.

Post-Spawn
- Weedy breaklines adjacent to spawning areas.
- Shallow, weedy humps near shore.
- Deep holes in spawning bays.

Summer and Early Fall
- Beneath matted weeds.
- Beneath shady docks.
- Weed flats near a drop-off.
- Gradually sloping points.
- Extended lips of points.
- Points and inside turns on weedline.

Late Fall
- Steep drop-offs.
- Deep humps and reefs.
- Sharp inside turns along the breakline.
- Deep clumps of green weeds.

Warm, shallow bays draw bass in early spring.

Northern eutrophic lakes abound with a variety of bass foods including perch, shiners, small sunfish, bullheads and numerous other roughfish.

To be consistent bass producers, these lakes must have a maximum depth of at least 20 feet. Otherwise, they are subject to frequent winterkills.

Covered docks provide bass with shade during summer.

Gradually sloping points, especially those with gravelly bottoms, make prime summertime feeding areas.

Southern Eutrophic Lakes

This lake category includes some of the country's premier trophy-bass lakes. Although the majority of these lakes are quite small, covering only a few dozen acres, some are massive. Florida's Lake Okeechobee, for example, covers more than 400,000 acres.

Southern eutrophic lakes are usually very shallow, with a maximum depth of 10 feet or less. The water clarity is low to moderate and the water often has a tannic (coffee-colored) stain. The warm, fertile water literally teems with bass foods such as shad, golden shiners, killifish and small sunfish.

Because most of these lakes are so shallow and exposed to the wind, they do not develop a thermocline. The water circulates completely, meaning that the water temperature is uniform from top to bottom.

Many of these lakes have vegetation of some type from shore to shore. You'll find extensive stands of floating-leaved plants like lily pads and water hyacinth, emergents like bulrushes and maidencane, and submergents like hydrilla.

The water temperature does not fluctuate nearly as much as in northern eutrophic lakes, so seasonal movement patterns are not as dramatic. Once the bass complete spawning and set up in their summer locations, they move very little until the following spring.

Largemouth Bass Locations in Southern Eutrophic Lakes During ...

Pre-Spawn/Spawn
- Boat canals cut through lakeshore property.

- Boat channels cut through emergent vegetation.
- Boat harbors.

- Patches of maidencane, cattails or peppergrass.
- Shallow bulrush beds.

Maidencane makes excellent spawning cover.

Boat canals warm quickly and attract pre-spawn bass.

Post-Spawn through Winter
- Main-lake hydrilla beds, especially isolated clumps.

- Deep bulrush beds.
- Beneath hyacinth and other matted weeds.

- Around stands of cypress trees.
- The same boat canals used at spawning time.

Hydrilla beds offer ample shade in summer.

The root system of a cypress tree creates good bass cover most of the year.

Meso Lakes

The term "meso" is short for mesotrophic, meaning medium fertility. Most everything else about these lakes is "medium" as well, including water temperature, clarity, depth and weed growth.

Although the majority of meso lakes are in the North, some can be found in the South as well. Many of the deep "sinkhole" lakes in Florida, for example, are classified as meso lakes.

In northern meso lakes, the primary forage for largemouth includes yellow perch, sunfish and a variety of small minnows, primarily shiners. The food supply in southern meso lakes is similar to that in southern eutrophic lakes (p. 38).

Because of their depth, these lakes have weed growth only in a band along the shoreline or on shallow humps. There are considerable areas of open water with a clean bottom.

The majority of these lakes stratify into distinct temperature layers during the summer months. The depths usually run out of oxygen by late summer, so bass do not have the option of going deep to find food or to avoid the summer heat.

Largemouth Bass Locations in Meso Lakes During ...

Pre-Spawn
- Soft-bottomed, cattail-fringed bays.
- Boat channels off the main lake.

Spawn
- Shallow bulrush points.
- Sandy bays, preferably those with woody cover.

Post-Spawn
- Shallow weed flats.
- Breaklines adjacent to spawning bays.

Shallow, muddy bays fringed with cattails attract bass before spawning.

Shallow bulrush points make prime spawning areas.

Summer and Early Fall
- Extended lips of points.
- Shallow weedy humps and flats.
- Slop bays.
- Docks adjacent to deep water.
- Inside weedlines.
- Irregular deepwater weedlines.

Late Fall and Winter
- Sharp-sloping points.
- Deep holes.
- Sharp inside turns on weedline.

Look for points with extended lips to find summer and fall bass.

Deepwater weedlines, especially those with an irregular edge, hold bass from summer through late fall.

Farm ponds built by damming a creek are much deeper at the dam end (a) than at the inflow end (b), as shown in the inset. In many cases, fill for the dam is excavated from the basin of the pond, leaving a deep trench (c) at the base of the dam. During most of the year, the weedy area of the pond holds the most bass, but the deep trench provides a coolwater retreat in summer and makes a good wintering area.

PONDS & PITS

Although you don't hear too much about these small man-made lakes, they provide a tremendous amount of quality bass fishing. In the United States alone, there are several million ponds, pits and quarries covering about 20 million acres.

A pond could be defined as a small man-made lake built to hold water for agricultural purposes, such as watering cattle, or for recreational purposes, such as fishing. In contrast, pits are merely holes in the ground that fill with water once the gravel, coal or minerals have been removed.

On the pages that follow are the types of small man-made lakes best suited for largemouth bass.

Farm Ponds

Often called "stock tanks," farm ponds are constructed for watering livestock, irrigating crops or controlling ero-

In the North, shallow farm ponds are prone to winterkill; many landowners now aerate their ponds in winter to keep the fish alive.

Gravel Pits

Gravel pits lack the fertility of farm ponds, so their water tends to be much clearer, with minimal weed growth. Many are stocked with largemouth, but the fish grow slowly and seldom reach a large size.

With the lack of cover, fishing may be tough because there is nothing to concentrate the bass. Fishing can be improved, however, by adding brush piles or other types of fish shelters.

Some gravel pits have steep-sided basins and are too deep and cold for largemouth. Such waters are better managed for trout.

sion. Besides largemouth, these ponds are often stocked with sunfish and, sometimes, catfish. Farm ponds are made by bulldozing or blasting a depression in the ground or building an earthen dam across a creek.

Because these ponds are usually on fertile soil, they have lush weed growth and an abundance of food. Bass grow rapidly, but if too many of them are removed by anglers, the sunfish tend to take over and become stunted.

Gravel pits are usually deep, clear and lack structure and cover, so look for largemouth on ledges, in shady indentations in the pit walls and around any fallen trees, brush piles or artificial fish shelter you can find. Find cover and you'll find bass.

Borrow Pits

Found along public highways, borrow pits remain after fill has been removed for road construction. They are usually shallower than gravel pits and have a rectangular shape, straight shorelines and a relatively flat bottom. Many have been stocked with a combination of largemouth bass and sunfish but, because of their lack of structure, good bass habitat is in short supply.

Strip Pits

After coal has been strip-mined, the abandoned pits fill with water and are often stocked with largemouth bass and sunfish. Some strip pits are also stocked with catfish, and a few deeper ones, with trout.

In some cases, new strip pits are too acidic to support fish. But after a few years, the acidity declines enough that stocked fish will survive.

Strip pits are most common in the East and Midwest. Some are more than a mile in length, with depths exceeding 50 feet. The sides are usually quite steep. Weedy or woody cover is minimal, so strip pits generally require extensive habitat improvement to support good gamefish populations. Improvements may include brush piles, fish shelters or even artificial reefs.

The straight sides and flat bottom of a borrow pit do not provide the habitat needed to support a large bass population.

Many years after mining has ceased, strip pits de-acidify and often produce decent bass crops.

Phosphate Pits

If you're lucky enough to know someone who owns a phosphate pit, you could be in for a largemouth bass bonanza. These highly fertile waters produce larger bass than any other type of pond or pit.

Phosphate pits, which are most common in Florida, remain after the phosphoric acid (used in farm fertilizers) has been removed. They are larger than most other kinds of ponds or pits, usually measuring from 40 to 150 acres and, occasionally, more than 1,000 acres.

The extremely high phosphate level in the water causes dense algal blooms that result in an abundance of baitfish and tremendous crops of fast-growing largemouth. Some phosphate pits are also stocked with bluegills, redear sunfish and catfish.

The best phosphate pits have an irregular shoreline and bottom, plenty of submerged or floating-leaved plants and a maximum depth of 30 to 50 feet. In shallower pits, the wind keeps the fertile bottom materials in suspension, sometimes resulting in a shortage of dissolved oxygen.

A phosphate pit's green water is the result of the high phosphate content. Bass grow rapidly in the fertile water.

RIVERS & STREAMS

Although largemouth bass are not normally considered "river fish," many warmwater rivers and streams support good largemouth crops. But for a river or stream to be a good bass producer, it must have plenty of slack-water habitat, such as slow pools or connecting sloughs and back-water lakes.

You can find largemouth in moving waters ranging in size from quiet streams only a few steps across to huge main-stem rivers that gather the flow from all other rivers and streams in a given drainage system.

Here are the main types of rivers and streams of interest to largemouth fishermen.

Small Streams

Unlike most big rivers, small streams do not have extensive backwater areas, so bass spend their entire lives within the confines of a rela-tively narrow channel. Look for them in pools and eddies or behind various types of current breaks.

Most small streams have an

Largemouth Bass Locations in Small Streams During ...

Pre-Spawn/Spawn
- Slack-water areas formed by indentations in the bank.
- Sandy shelves on downstream ends of islands.
- Shallow sand-gravel shoals on inside bends.
- Around fallen trees and log-jams in shallow water.

Look for bass in slow, weedy stretches from late spring through mid-fall.

Post-Spawn through Mid-Fall
- Around logjams, beaver lodges and fallen trees in deep water.
- Deep pools.
- Eddies below points, boulders and bridge pilings.
- Holes below sandbars.
- Undercut banks.
- Tailwaters of low-head dams.
- Slow-moving reaches with submerged vegetation.

Late Fall and Winter
- Deepest pools in the stream.
- Deep pools in larger rivers into which the stream flows.

Eddies below bridge pilings are prime summertime bass hangouts.

Logjams and beaver lodges break the current and provide shade for summertime largemouth.

abundance of bass food, such as shiners, chubs, dace and other creek minnows, as well as crayfish.

Many good largemouth streams also support small-mouth bass, sunfish and crappies, in addition to suckers, redhorse and other roughfish. Some even have walleyes.

Big Rivers

Mainstem rivers with extensive backwater systems make superb habitat for largemouth bass. Weedy sloughs and shallow lakes connected to the main channel provide bass cover similar to that found in many natural lakes, and the side channels, or cuts, leading into the backwaters also hold good numbers of bass.

But big rivers can be difficult to fish. Besides the weedy cover, there is an abundance of woody cover, as well as a good deal of manmade cover, where the fish can hide. Because the water is often muddy, you'll have to get your bait close to the fish to draw a strike. To further complicate matters, the water level fluctuates greatly, making it difficult to establish a consistent pattern.

Not only are big rivers highly fertile, they support an extremely diverse collection of fish life. So largemouth have plenty to eat, but they must also compete with a lot of other predator fish—like smallmouth bass, walleyes, northern pike, catfish and white bass—for the available food.

Rivers that are confined by levees seldom produce as many bass as rivers that are allowed to spread freely over the floodplain. They lack the diverse habitat needed for a healthy gamefish crop.

Largemouth Bass Locations in Big Rivers During ...

Pre-Spawn/Spawn
- "Dead" sloughs with plenty of vegetation.
- Weedy fringes of backwater lakes.
- Shallow stump fields.
- Islands of emergent vegetation in backwaters.
- Side channels with slow current and woody cover.

Post-Spawn through Mid-Fall
- Deep, weedy backwater lakes.
- Weedy main-channel wing-dams with slow current.
- Deep eddies at the head of an island.
- Riprap with slow current.
- Side channels with slow current and woody cover.

Late Fall
- Shallow weed flats in backwaters on warm, sunny days.
- Side channels with slow current and woody cover.

Winter
- Shallow weed flats in backwaters at first ice.
- Deep holes in backwaters in midwinter.

Shallow stump fields in backwaters make good spawning sites. Deeper stumps may hold bass all summer.

Slow-moving side channels with fallen trees and other woody cover hold largemouth most of the year.

Backwater lakes with deep water and lush weed growth make ideal bass habitat from spring through fall.

A stretch of riprap with slow current and weedy cover holds largemouth in summer and fall.

Tidewater Rivers

Compared to most other freshwater fish, largemouth have a high salt tolerance, so they thrive in the brackish estuaries formed by coastal rivers flowing into the sea.

Tidewater rivers usually support more and bigger largemouth than similar rivers fed only by freshwater. The bass not only have access to most of the usual freshwater foods, they can also partake of the abundant supply of marine life, including shrimp, crabs and anadromous baitfish such as herring.

Most tidal rivers have numerous backwater areas connected to the main channel by chutes, giving bass the varied habitat they prefer.

But fishing a tidewater river is even more of a challenge than fishing a big freshwater river. Anglers must time their fishing to the tides and know where to look for bass at different tidal stages. On an incoming tide, for example, bass usually hold on the inside of a chute, waiting for the current to deliver food. But on an outgoing tide, they're more likely to be on the river side of the chute so they don't get trapped by the falling water.

Largemouth Bass Locations in Tidewater Rivers During ...

Pre-Spawn/Spawn
- Deeper channels through rice fields and other shallow, weedy flats.
- Chutes leading into weedy backwaters.
- Back ends of weedy backwaters.
- Man-made boat channels.
- Small tributaries.

Post-Spawn through Mid-Fall
- Chutes leading into backwater lakes.
- Matted weeds in backwater lakes.
- Stick-ups and other woody cover in backwater lakes.
- Deep channels in backwater lakes.
- Wooden bridge pilings in main channel.

Late Fall and Winter
- Chutes leading into backwater lakes.
- Deep holes in main channel adjacent to backwater lakes.
- Deep holes along outside bends in main channel.

Look for stick-ups in shallow backwaters to find summertime bass.

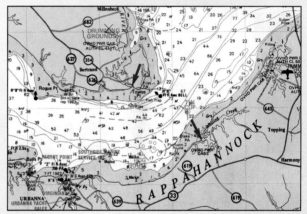
Chutes leading into weedy backwaters (arrows) hold largemouth most of the year.

Weedy cover in backwater lakes attracts largemouth from spring through fall.

Deep channels in backwater lakes give summertime bass a resting area.

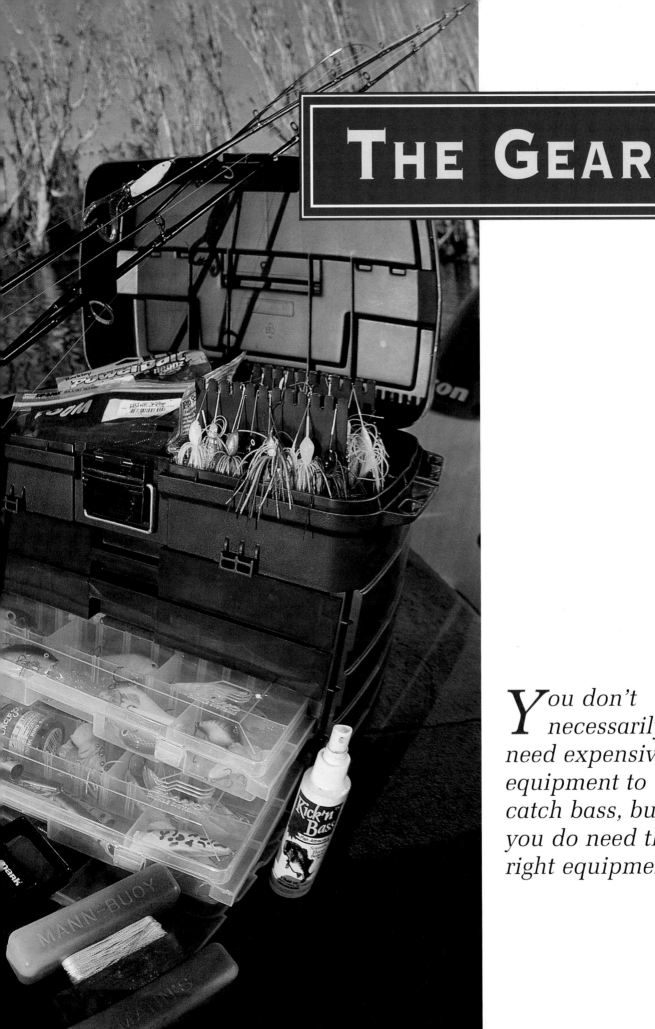

THE GEAR

*Y*ou don't necessarily need expensive equipment to catch bass, but you do need the right equipment.

BASS BOATS

You don't need a glitzy bass boat to catch largemouth, but there's no arguing the fact that boats designed specifically for bass fishing will help you fish more effectively in most situations.

If you're a serious bass angler, here's why you should consider investing in a bass boat:

• It will get you to your fishing spot in a hurry, a big advantage—especially if you're a tournament angler.
• Bass boats have a shallow-draft hull that enables you to get into shallow, weedy bays and other spots that would be inaccessible with a deep-V hull.
• The low-profile design and elevated casting decks make casting easier. The low profile also improves boat control by minimizing the effects of the wind on the hull.
• The wide hull is extremely stable, enabling you to safely stand up in the boat while casting.

Although you can buy a bass boat only 16 feet long

Types of Bass Boats

Aluminum bass boats range in length from 16 to 19 feet and are designed for 30 to 150 hp outboards. They are considerably less expensive than fiberglass boats, but their ride is not as smooth.

Mid-size fiberglass bass boats range in length from 16 to 18 feet and are powered by outboards from 50 to 125 hp. They are well suited for the majority of bass-fishing situations.

Large fiberglass bass boats, sometimes referred to as "aircraft carriers," may be more than 20 feet long and 7½ feet wide at the transom. They accommodate outboards from 150 to 225 hp. These boats carry more gear, have a larger fuel capacity and handle bigger waters than mid-size models.

powered by an outboard as small as 30 hp, the current trend is toward bigger, more powerful, faster boats. Some manufacturers offer boats more than 20 feet long designed for outboards up to 225 hp. These rigs skip across the water at speeds of up to 70 mph.

Rod lockers should be at least 7 feet in length or longer if you use longer rods. The boat should also be equipped with Velcro straps, for securing rods on high-speed runs.

Insulated, aerated live wells keep your fish alive indefinitely. Without insulation, the water may heat up and stress the fish. Live wells with timers give you intermittent aeration, saving battery power.

Storage compartments should have watertight lids to prevent mildew of clothing and life jackets, and rusting of expensive tackle. Battery compartments should hold 2 or 3 full-size marine batteries.

A bilge pump is a must for safety and optimal performance. Some boats have both an automatic pump that turns on whenever there is water in the hull and a switch-operated backup pump.

A bow-mount trolling motor with manual steering is more reliable than one with a foot control.

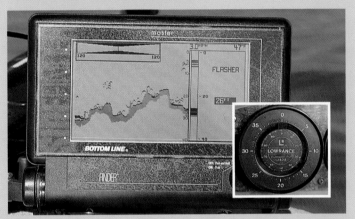

Depth finders are a must for most types of bass fishing. Many anglers prefer an in-dash flasher (inset) for high-speed sounding and a bow-mounted LCD for fishing purposes.

Power trim maximizes high-speed performance by keeping your bow at the right angle regardless of your load. Power tilt enables you to lift your motor enough to negotiate extremely shallow water.

Elevated casting decks in the bow and stern make casting easier. And because you're sitting so high, you can see into the water more easily. Some anglers prefer swivel chairs; others, butt seats.

Optional Bass Boat Features

Onboard battery chargers are a great convenience because they enable you to charge all your boat's batteries at once. Just attach an extension cord to a plug inside the boat.

A weather-band radio is recommended if you'll be running long distances on big water. Some anglers also carry a marine radio, so they can contact a marina or other anglers in case of emergency.

High-performance props get your boat "out of the hole" faster, give it extra stability and make it handle better. They are usually a little larger than ordinary props and may have 4 or more blades, rather than the normal 3.

A foot pedal leaves both hands free for steering and makes it easier to decelerate quickly in case of emergency.

A welded frame is quieter, stronger and more maintenance-free than one held together with bolts. A bolted frame loosens with use, developing rattles and requiring periodic tightening.

Fiberglass bass boats usually require a bunk trailer. On most roller trailers, the rollers do not have enough surface area to support the boat's weight, so they may cause serious damage to the hull.

Wheel hubs should have grease zerts that enable you to periodically add bearing grease. This forces out any water that may have seeped in and it reduces the frequency of wheel-bearing maintenance.

A tongue jack makes it easy to lift your trailer onto and off your trailer hitch.

U-shaped float tubes are gaining in popularity, mainly because they have an open-ended design that makes it easier to get in and out.

Float Tubes & Inflatable Boats

Countless anglers do much of their bass fishing in farm ponds, gravel pits, small streams or other waters where launching and fishing from a full-sized boat would be impossible.

You could use a small car-top boat or canoe to fish these waters, but many fishermen prefer float tubes or inflatable boats because they are even lighter and more portable.

Float tubes consist of a rubber innertube or a U-shaped urethane or vinyl bladder covered with a heavy-duty nylon shell. Most have a nylon seat and some type of backrest. Float tubes are usually propelled by kick fins worn on the angler's feet, but some can be outfitted with a small electric trolling motor.

Most inflatable boats are made of tough, heavy-duty PVC. Not only are they very puncture-resistant, most also have several air compartments. This way, even if one compartment gets punctured, the craft will still stay afloat. Inflatable boats usually come with lightweight aluminum or plastic oars, but some models can accommodate small outboard motors. Most models have inflatable seats and some have rigid floorboards.

Float tubes and inflatable boats can be blown up with a hand pump or an electric air pump that plugs into the cigarette lighter of your car.

Here are the most common types of float tubes and inflatable boats, along with some handy accessories.

Popular Types of Inflatables

Donut-shaped tubes are kept afloat by a single tire inner tube. These tubes are inexpensive, but climbing in and out of them may be difficult.

Pontoon-style "kick-boats" have two separate air chambers. Should one chamber spring a leak, the other will still keep you afloat.

Large inflatables outfitted with outboard motors are necessary for fishing larger waters or for traveling long distances. Most have several air chambers. These boats vary in length from 8 to 12 feet, weigh 25 to 50 pounds and can carry 2 to 5 passengers.

Accessories for Float Tubes & Inflatable Boats

Kick fins used to propel float tubes and kick boats should fit over stocking-foot waders. This way, you'll be able to fish in cool water.

A small anchor comes in handy for holding your position when fishing in a float tube. This model weighs only 1½ pounds.

A depth-finder mounted on your float tube enables you to check the depth and look for fish.

ELECTRIC TROLLING MOTORS

A serious bass angler would find it nearly impossible to fish without a good electric trolling motor. Not only does a trolling motor give you precise boat control, it enables you to hover silently over fish in open water and it will get you into shallow or weedy bass hideouts that would be inaccessible with most outboards. If you're using a small boat or inflatable, a trolling motor may be your only means of propulsion.

As important as a trolling motor is to your bass-fishing success, it pays to select a top-quality model with all of the features you need for your type of fishing. Here are some guidelines for making the right selection:

• **Thrust.** This is the most important consideration in selecting a trolling motor. If your motor does not have adequate thrust, you won't be able to hold your boat in the wind. And when you get blown off your spot, you'll spend too much time trying to get back on it.

How much thrust you need depends on the weight of your boat (refer to table at right). These recommendations are considerably higher than those of most manufacturers, but it doesn't pay to scrimp on thrust.

Trolling motors are available in 12-, 24- and 36-volt models that require 1, 2 or 3 12-volt batteries, respectively. Some models can operate on two different voltages, either 12 and 24 or 24 and 36. As a rule, higher-voltage models draw less amperage, so they run for a longer time on the same battery setup.

• **Front or Rear.** If you own a small boat without a front deck, or if your trolling motor is your sole means of propulsion, a transom-mount trolling motor is the best choice. On bass boats or other boats with a front deck, most anglers prefer a bow-mount motor. A bow-mount is easier to steer and many models have controls (opposite)

Recommended Thrust

Boat Weight* (Pounds)	Pounds of Thrust
600	30
1000	40
1250	50
1500	60
2000	70 or more

*Includes passengers and gear

- **Steering Control.** Most transom-mount electrics and some bow-mounts are operated by a hand control, ensuring trouble-free performance.

The majority of bow-mount trolling motors are controlled by a foot pedal connected to the motor by a cable. Some models, however, feature electronic steering mechanisms controlled by a radio signal or human voice, so no cumbersome cable is necessary. A few models have an "autopilot" feature that steers the boat on a selected heading, even in a strong wind.

- **Speed Control.** Inexpensive trolling motors often come with a control that gives you a choice of several fixed speeds. Most serious bass anglers, however, prefer a variable-speed motor because it enables them to make fine adjustments in their speed to compensate for the wind and current.

Most variable speed controls come with a pulse-width modulator that not only gives you an infinite range of speeds, it also improves your motor's efficiency and greatly extends battery life.

that leave your hands free for fishing.

Trolling Motor Tips

Look for a motor with a composite (rather than metal) shaft that will flex but not bend or break if you hit a log or other solid object. The shaft should be long enough so your prop is at least 7 inches beneath the water's surface.

For fishing in heavy vegetation, choose a motor with a weedless prop. The hub of the prop should fit flush with the housing of the motor. If there is a gap or indentation between the two, weeds will collect in the opening.

If you'll be fishing in heavy cover, be sure to choose a motor with a heavy-duty mounting bracket. Some top-of-the-line brackets have a breakaway feature that allows the shaft to "give" when you strike a solid object.

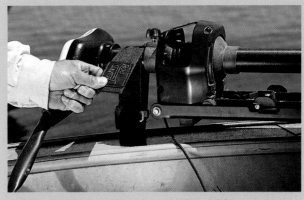

A bow-mount trolling motor should have a tie-down strap or bar to secure it on high-speed runs in rough water. Otherwise, the motor could bounce up and come down in the water.

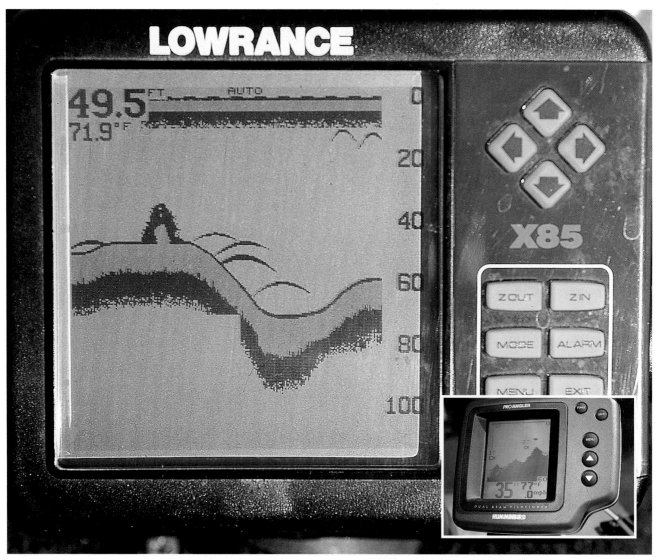

Liquid-crystal sonar units display fish and other objects as a group of pixels. In a high-quality unit, the image consists of more pixels and has greater detail than on an inexpensive unit (inset).

ELECTRONICS

A quick glance at the interior of a well-equipped bass boat will give you a pretty good idea of the importance of modern electronics. Here are some of the items you're likely to see:

Depth Finders

Most successful bass anglers will tell you that they rely more heavily on their depth finder than on any other piece of equipment in their boat. In fact, many bass-fishing boats are equipped with a pair of depth finders, one on the console and one on the front deck. Not only will a good depth finder help get you to your spot without running into a reef or other underwater obstruction, it will quickly help you find the most productive structure and pinpoint the fish.

Here are the most impor-tant considerations in selecting a depth finder:

• **Type of Display.** All depth finders operate on the same principle: A transducer emits a sonar signal that bounces off bottom, weeds, timber, fish or other objects. The time it takes the returning echo to reach the transducer is a measure of the object's depth. The sonar signal may be displayed on a liquid-crystal or video screen, or on a flasher dial.

Liquid-crystal recorders (LCRs) dominate the market. They have a display consisting of tiny "pixels." The more pixels per unit area of the screen, the better the resolution. A good unit generally has a vertical pixel count of at least 160, and the best units have more than 200. Liquid-crystals are not recommended at temperatures below 20°F, however, because the signal is slow to appear on the screen.

Video recorders provide the best resolution of any depth finder. The signal is displayed on a cathode-ray tube (CRT) like that of a TV set. Monochrome videos display the signal in a single color. Color videos show different size targets in different colors. The main drawbacks of videos are that they are bulky and hard to read in direct sun.

Flashers display a momentary signal on a round dial. Many anglers prefer flashers for high-speed sounding, because flashers give a real-time depth reading. But flashers also work well for finding fish. Because the signal is not recorded on a screen, however, you must watch closely or you may not see the fish.

Most flashers display the signal in a single color, but multicolor flashers are available. They display signals in different colors, depending on target size and position in the cone. But color flashers are hard to read in direct sunlight.

Liquid-crystal flashers have a black-and-white display that is easy to read on a

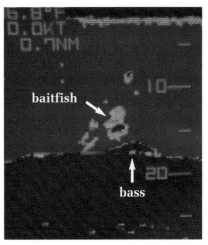

Color videos make it possible to distinguish small targets, such as baitfish (blue marks), from larger ones such as bass (red mark). In addition, the resolution of a video is superior to that of an LCD.

sunny day, and they have a backlit dial for night fishing.

Color flashers also make it easy to distinguish baitfish (green lines) from larger fish (red lines). But in bright sunlight, you'll need some type of hood (inset) to shade the dial.

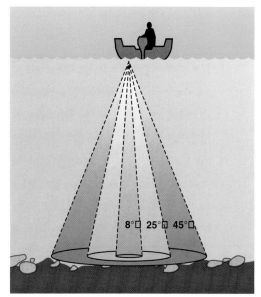

The cone angle of your transducer determines how much of the bottom you can see on the screen or dial. As a rule, the diameter of the circle covered by an 8° cone is about 1/6 of the depth; a 25° cone, about 1/2 of the depth and a 45° cone, about the same as the depth. So if you're fishing in 20 feet of water with an 8° transducer, you're covering a circle with a diameter of 3-4 feet; with a 25°, 10-11 feet and a 45°, about 20 feet.

• **Cone Angle of Transducer.** Most depth-finder manufacturers offer a choice of transducers, at least for their top-quality units. For example, you may be able to buy a 50, 120 or 200 kHz transducer for the same unit. A 50 kHz transducer emits a cone of sound that spreads at an angle of up to 45°; a 120 kHz, 25-30° and a 200 kHz, as little as 8°.

Although many anglers pay little attention to this detail, they really should. As a rule, the narrower the cone angle, the better your "target separation." This improves your chances of being able to see individual fish in a school, rather than a single mass of fish, and it will help you detect fish lying close to the bottom. A wider cone is a better choice when you're scouting for fish, because it allows you to see more of the bottom. It also works better in very deep water.

Some top-shelf units have dual-beam transducers and a switch that enables you to choose between a wide beam and a narrow beam.

• **Sweep Speed.** The rate at which the "picture" travels across the screen of an LCD or video is called the "sweep speed" or "chart speed." Again, this is a detail that most anglers overlook, but it can make a big difference in your fishing.

The sweep speed is adjustable on most sonar units. If the top-end sweep speed is high enough, you can run your boat at high speed and still graph fish. But if the top-end speed is too slow, the marks will not be wide enough to interpret.

Videos generally have a much higher top-end sweep speed than LCDs. If you prefer an LCD, make sure the sweep speed is fast enough that fish marks are recognizable at a moderate boat speed. When comparing units, test them in "simulator" mode; some have considerably faster sweep speeds than others.

Importance of Sweep Speed

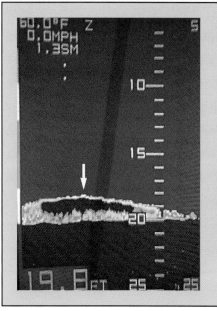

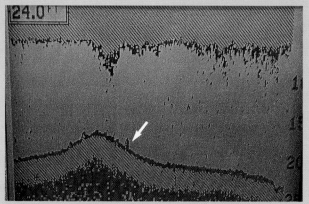

Fast Sweep Speed. *The signal is "stretched out" on the screen, so you can tell what it is even when the boat is moving fast. On this video screen, it's obvious that the mark (arrow) is a fish.*

Slow Sweep Speed. *A fish makes only a very narrow mark when your boat passes over it at high speed. It is impossible to tell if the mark on this LCD screen (arrow) is a fish or a bit of debris on the bottom.*

GPS Navigators

Bass anglers who spend a lot of time fishing large waters, such as sprawling southern reservoirs or big natural lakes, rely heavily on GPS navigators to help them unerringly reach their fishing destinations, even at night, in dense fog or under other low-visibility conditions.

GPS, which stands for Global Positioning System, operates on signals received from a network of satellites that circle the earth.

In addition to its obvious value in finding fishing spots, GPS also can be used as an invisible marker. On most popular fishing waters, tossing out a marker buoy is like waving a flag that says "Come and fish right here." With your GPS unit in plotter mode, you can easily monitor the position of your boat in relation to a spot where you caught fish, and nobody will know your secret.

For many popular fishing waters, you can buy maps or logs that show GPS coordinates for the best fishing spots. Some higher-priced GPS units accommodate map modules that show prominent lake features, such as points and islands, that can help in navigation. Maps showing depth contours are available for certain large lakes, and more maps of this type will soon be available.

GPS is also a great safety device. If you remember to punch in the location of the boat landing before you embark, you can always find your way back, even in a severe thunderstorm or thick fog. If you fish on a large lake studded with dangerous reefs, you can use your GPS to make a "route" that enables you to safely travel to your fishing spot without wiping out your lower unit. When you reach the first point on the route, the unit automati-cally switches to the second, keeping you off the reefs and leading you to your destination in step-by-step fashion, even on days when you can't see the bow of your boat. The route can be reversed when you want to return to your starting point.

Handheld, battery-powered GPS units are surprisingly inexpensive, and they seem to be just as accurate as the permanent-mount units that operate off your boat's 12-volt electrical system and sell for double to triple the price. But handhelds have a small screen that may be difficult to read, especially in plotter mode.

Whatever type of unit you prefer, make sure it has a parallel-channel receiver capable of simultaneously tracking signals from at least 12 satellites. This type of receiver will process data quickly and accurately.

Basic Types of GPS Units

Permanent-Mount. *These units operate off your boat's 12-volt power system. They have a considerably larger screen than that of a handheld unit, so they are easier to read.*

Handheld. *Handhelds are popular because of their portability and low cost. But the small screen is a drawback, especially when the unit is in plotter mode.*

Steering Arrow. *A steering arrow makes it easy to find your waypoint; you simply keep the arrow pointing straight ahead and watch your DTG (distance to go) until it reaches zero.*

Plotter Screen. *With the unit in plotter mode, you can visually track the boat's path in relation to your waypoint, rather than relying on a confusing numeric display.*

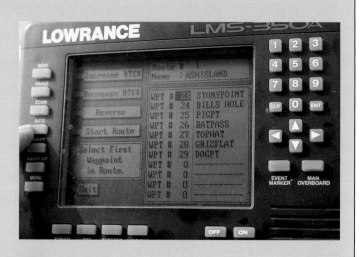

Route Planning. *You can navigate more safely in reef-studded lakes by following a route consisting of several waypoints. When you reach the first waypoint, the unit automatically switches to the second, etc.*

Mapping. *A mapping GPS unit is a valuable navigation aid. Some units accept map cartridges; others have a port for downloading mapping data from a personal computer.*

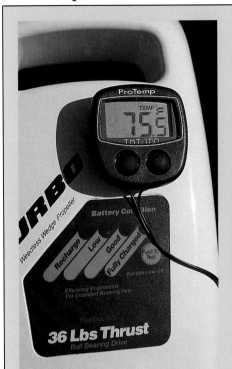

Electric Thermometer. *To measure water temperature beneath the surface, you'll need an electric thermometer with a temperature probe attached to a long cord.*

Surface Temperature Gauge. *This stand-alone surface temperature gauge has a sensor that attaches to your trolling motor's lower unit.*

Marine-Band Radio. *A marine radio enables you to exchange fishing information with other anglers and to get help in case of emergency. It also provides weather information.*

Underwater Video Camera. *These small, waterproof video cameras take the guesswork out of finding fish and determining what type of structure they're using. They come equipped with an extra-wide-angle lens and a fin on the back to keep the camera pointing in the direction the boat is moving. The camera is lowered to the desired depth on an insulated cable that connects it to a monitor in the boat.*

MAPS

A good lake map or river chart will help put you on fish in a hurry—if you know how to read and interpret it properly.

Maps of most significant fishing waters are available from government agencies, such as state fish and game departments, the U.S. Army Corps of Engineers and the Tennessee Valley Authority (TVA). Many private mapping companies also offer a wide selection of maps, often with more detailed fishing information than those available from government agencies.

Here are some of the most common type of maps used by bass anglers:

Maps of Natural Lakes

Hydrographic maps of natural lakes are made by establishing a grid over the lake's surface and then sounding at intervals along the grid lines. While depths along the grid lines are fairly precise, the resulting map may not be as accurate as anglers would hope.

To produce a finished map, mapmakers estimate contour lines by "connecting the dots." In a complex basin, however, it's easy to connect the wrong dots, resulting in an inaccurate map. Another problem: The finished map may not show all of the lake's structure, because there could be humps and other structural elements *between* the grid lines.

Still, a lake map gives you a good starting point. When you find an inaccuracy or a piece of structure that doesn't show on your map, pencil in the changes. Eventually, you'll develop a more realistic version.

In recent years, a few natural lakes have been mapped with the aid of GPS and the resulting maps are highly accurate. GPS mapping will certainly become more prevalent in the future.

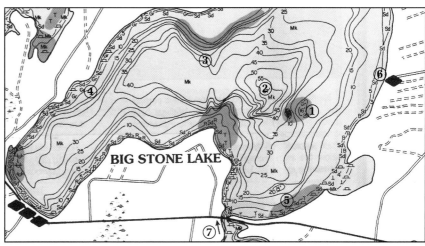

Maps of Natural Lakes. In addition to prominent features of the lake bottom such as (1) humps, (2) holes and (3) points, these maps may also show (4) bottom type, (5) weedbeds, (6) boat ramps and the location of (7) inlets and outlets.

Reservoir Maps

Because the topography of the land was well known at the time most reservoirs were filled, these maps are usually quite accurate. But reservoirs tend to silt in fairly rapidly, especially at their upper ends, so old maps may not

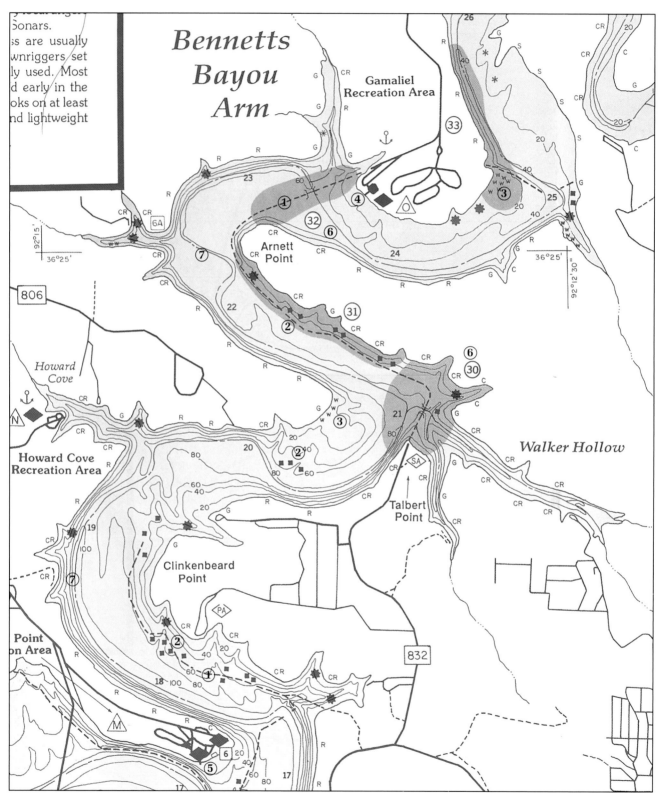

Reservoir Maps. *In addition to water depth, reservoir maps also show features such as (1) submerged roadbeds, (2) submerged building foundations, (3) stands of flooded timber, (4) boat ramps, (5) marinas, (6) locational markers and (7) river and creek channels.*

give you an accurate representation of the bottom contour.

Another consideration when using reservoir maps: The water level in a reservoir may vary tremendously over the course of the year, so bottom contours are sometimes listed in feet above sea level. To determine the actual depth at a point on this type of map, you'll have to subtract the bottom contour reading from the current pool elevation.

Many large reservoirs are quite complex, so government agencies often post signs on points, islands and other prominent features to serve as navigational aids. Should you get lost, all you have to do is find one of these signs and then look at your map to locate that number.

River Charts

The U.S. Army Corps of Engineers offers navigation charts for many mainstem rivers including the Mississippi, Missouri and Ohio rivers. The charts, which come in handy spiral-bound books, provide valuable fishing information, such as the location of sloughs, stump fields, riprap banks, wingdams and boat ramps.

The maps also give mileage readings along the main chan-

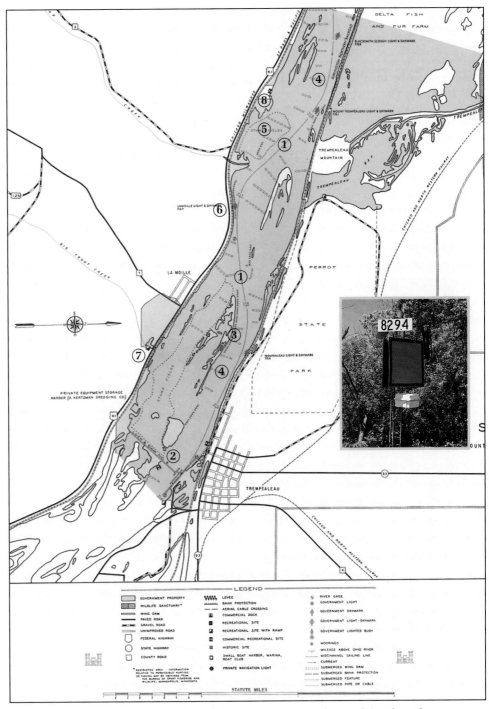

River Charts. *These maps show (1) the main river channel (with mileage marks), (2) locks and dams, (3) riprap banks, (4) wingdams, (5) stump fields, (6) daymarks with river mileage (inset), (7) boat ramps and (8) resorts.*

nel. On the water, you can compare these readings to the mileage shown on river daymarks, so you'll always know where you are.

Because depths in major rivers are constantly changing due to flooding, dredging and

fluctuations in current patterns, navigation charts normally do not show bottom contours. Unless you're familiar with a particular area, always motor slowly through any areas off the main river channel.

73

RODS & REELS

If you were to check the rod locker of a top bass pro, you'd probably find at least a half dozen rod-and-reel combos and maybe even a dozen. That's because the pros fish virtually every kind of bass water using a wide variety of lures and presentations.

Although the majority of today's bass rods are made of high-modulus graphite, which has a high stiffness-to-weight ratio, some anglers are turning to "softer" rods for specific purposes. When using "superlines," for example, a rod that is too stiff

A flippin' stick has the length to guide your lure into hard-to-reach spots and the power to horse bass out of a tangle of cover.

spooled with heavy mono (17- to 25-pound test) or superline. The heavy line is needed to minimize the number of break-offs and to horse bass out of dense cover before they can tangle your line around a branch.

But flippin' sticks are not just for flippin'. They also work well for distance casting, deep jigging, buzzbaiting and tossing very heavy lures, such as magnum plugs.

• **Pitchin' Rods.** These rods are used to make the low-trajectory, underhand casts

could snap on the hookset, so you may want to try a fiberglass or fiberglass-graphite composite rod.

Unless you fish bass for a living, you won't need all the rods described below, but you should probably have at least two or three of the following outfits:

• **Flippin' Sticks.** These long, heavy-power, fast-action rods are ideal for flipping jigs or soft plastics into pockets in the brush and other tight spots. Most are 7½ feet in length, too long for the average rod locker, so they are designed to telescope down to about 6½ feet.

Flippin' sticks are usually paired with a sturdy baitcasting reel

The narrow spool reel on a pitchin' outfit is ideal for making short, precise casts; it has less momentum than a wider and heavier spool so overruns are less likely.

A jig/worm rod has the "backbone" necessary to sink the hook, yet is sensitive enough to detect subtle strikes from finicky bass like this.

that are necessary to place lures under tree limbs, docks and other obstructions that are only a few inches above the water.

Rods used for pitchin' are about 6½ feet long with medium-heavy power and a fast action.

Because pitchin' involves very short casts, there is no need for a heavy, high-capacity reel. The best choice is a reel with a very narrow spool. A spool of this type has less momentum than a wider, heavier spool, so you can easily thumb it to drop your bait into a precise spot with less chance of a backlash.

Spinnerbait fishermen often use rods similar to those used for pitchin', but they substitute a wider-spool reel that enables them to make longer casts.

• **Jig/Worm Rod.** For casting or vertically jigging with jigs, bladebaits, tailspinners or other jig-

ging lures in the ⅜- to 1-ounce range, most experienced bass anglers prefer a 6½-foot, heavy-power, fast-action baitcaster with an

extra-long handle. The same type of rod works well for fishing Texas-rigged soft plastics.

The extra-stiff blank combined with the long handle provides the power necessary for making long casts. The power is also needed to sink a thick jig hook or to drive a worm hook through the plastic and into the jaw of a bass.

A jig/worm rod is usually paired with a sturdy baitcasting reel (gear-ratio of at least 6:1) spooled with 12- to 20-pound-test mono or 20- to 30-pound-test superline.

• **Crankbait/Topwater Rod.** When fishing with crankbaits or topwaters such as propbaits, stickbaits and chuggers, you need a rod with a fairly soft tip. This way, there is less resistance when a bass "sucks" in the bait, meaning it can take the lure deeper. A softer tip also slightly delays

A crankbait/topwater rod flexes enough at the tip to allow bass to "inhale" the bait without feeling much resistance.

A grub/tube rod has enough flex to "load" from the weight of a small jig, tubebait or other near-ly weightless lure.

the hookset, reducing the chances that you'll set too soon and pull the bait away from the fish.

A 6½-foot, medium-power, medium-action baitcaster makes a good all-around crankbait/topwater rod. Some crankbait anglers prefer fiber-glass rods because of their extra-soft tips.

For the long casts often needed with crankbaits and topwa-ters, use a wide-spool baitcasting reel.

• **Grub/Tube Rod.** Casting a grub body on a tiny jig head, a tubebait on a lightly weighted hook or other lightweight lure requires a spinning outfit and light mono, usually 6- to 8-pound test.

A typical grub/tube rod is about 6 feet long, with medium power and a fast action. Pair it with a medium-size, long-spool spinning reel with a gear ratio of at least 5:1.

Not only will this out-fit enable you to make lengthy casts with these light baits, it is ideal for making "skip casts" to place a bait under docks or overhangs.

• **Fly Rod.** The big, wind-resistant flies used for largemouth (pp. 127-128) require a 7- to 9-weight fly rod with a weight-forward or bass taper line. Your leader should be 6 to 9 feet in length with a 0X to 2X tippet.

A fly rod must be powerful enough to handle the heavy line needed to punch a bulky fly into the wind.

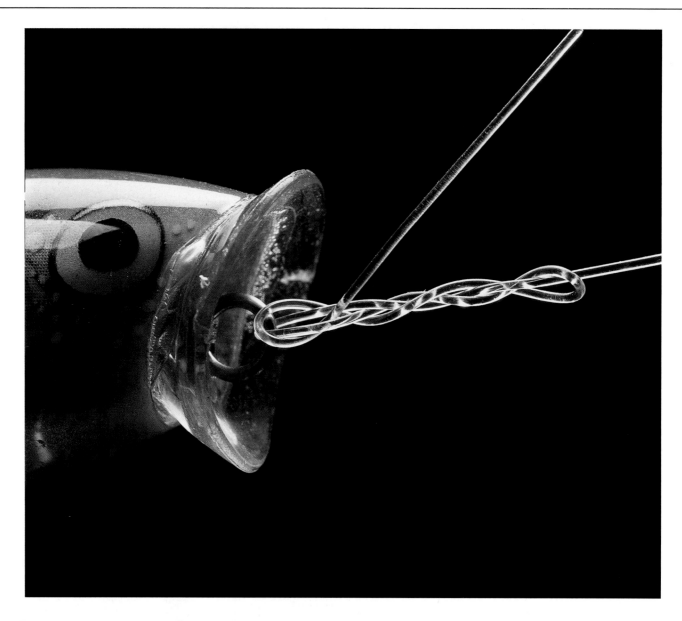

LINES & KNOTS

The average bass angler takes great pains to choose the perfect boat and motor and rig it with the latest electronic gadgetry, but line selection and knot tying usually rank much lower on the priority list.

Most of the time, this inattention to detail is of little consequence. When you're catching average-size bass, even cheap lines and poorly tied knots are not likely to fail. Only on rare occasion

will your line or knot give way: When you hook a trophy-caliber bass.

Modern bass anglers rely almost exclusively on two main types of line: monofilament and superline. Here are some tips for selecting the right lines and tying the best knots for your type of fishing.

Monofilament

Monofilament is still the most popular type of fishing

line. Not only is it relatively inexpensive, it can be used for practically any kind of bass fishing. Of course, it has one big advantage over other kinds of fishing lines: It is nearly invisible in the water.

But mono has several drawbacks. It is relatively stiff and tends to take a set if it is not used frequently. Old line comes off the spool in coils, seriously limiting casting performance.

Nylon stretches more than

other line materials; some mono stretches as much as 30 percent. This much stretch can make it difficult to set the hook, especially when you're fishing in deep water.

The amino acids in nylon are easily damaged by ultraviolet rays from the sun. Leaving your reels exposed to sunlight too long may weaken your line.

Monofilament lines made from a single type of nylon are generally inferior to *copolymer* lines, which are a blend of two or more types of nylon. Copolymers have qualities that are impossible to attain with only one type of nylon. For example, by combining nylon materials with different characteristics, manufacturers can create lines that have lower-than-normal stretch, more abrasion resistance or more tensile strength (strength for the diameter) than ordinary mono.

Superlines

Made of superstrong polyethylene fibers, "superlines" have extraordinary tensile strength, meaning that they are extremely strong for their diameter. They have practically no stretch, so they give you incredible "feel," enabling you to detect the most subtle strikes. And because they have no memory (tendency to form coils), you won't have to change line after not using your rod for a few months.

On the downside, superlines are considerably more expensive than mono. They are easily weakened by abrasion with sharp-edged rocks. The lack of memory may cause ugly snarls. If you get a serious backlash, you may have no choice but to get out your knife and start cutting. The low stretch factor can also be a detriment. It may cause you to pull the bait away from the fish too soon and, if you set the hook too hard, you could snap your rod.

Tying knots in superline, which has a very slick surface, can be a problem. Unless you use the right knots, they could cut into themselves or slip.

There are two basic types of superline: braided and fused. Braided lines may or may not have an outer coating to contain the fibers. Fused lines are heat-treated to thermally bond the fibers.

Fused lines are stiffer and have more memory, but they have better knot strength and are more abrasion-resistant.

Refer to the "Line-Selection Chart" (below) to help select the right type of line for your fishing, and refer to "Important Bass-Fishing Knots" (pp. 80-81) for instructions on tying the right knots.

Line-Selection Chart

PROPERTY	TYPE OF LINE								
	MONOFILAMENT			BRAIDED SUPERLINE			FUSED SUPERLINE		
	Low	Med	High	Low	Med	High	Low	Med	High
Knot Strength			X	X				X	
Tensile Strength	X					X			X
Abrasion Resistance			X	X				X	
Stiffness			X	X				X	
Stretch			X	X			X		
Visibility	X				X			X	
Memory		X		X				X	

Important Bass-Fishing Knots

Attaching Line to Spool—Mono or Superline: Arbor Knot

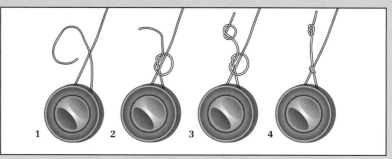

The arbor knot is so named because it tightens firmly around the arbor, preventing the line from slipping when you reel.

(1) Pass the line around the spool; **(2)** wrap the free end around the standing line and make an overhand knot; **(3)** make an overhand knot in the free end; **(4)** snug up the knot by pulling on the standing line; the knot should tighten firmly around the arbor.

Attaching Hook or Lure—Mono or Superline: Trilene Knot

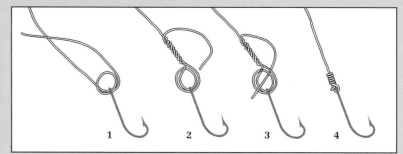

The Trilene knot has a double loop around the hook eye and is one of the strongest hook-attachment knots.

(1) Form a double loop by passing the free end through the hook eye twice; **(2)** wrap the free end around the standing line 4-5 times; **(3)** pass the free end through the double loop; **(4)** pull on the standing line and hook to snug up the knot.

Attaching Hook or Lure—Mono or Superline: Palomar Knot

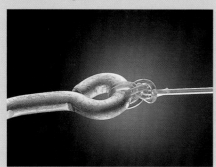

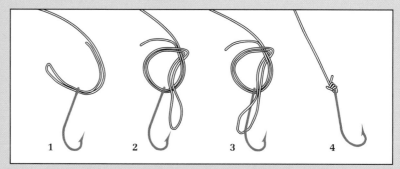

The palomar knot, like the Trilene knot, has a double loop around the hook eye. But some anglers find it easier to tie.

(1) Form a double line, then push it through the hook eye; **(2)** with the double line, make an overhand knot around the standing line and free end; **(3)** put the hook through the loop; **(4)** hold the hook while pulling on the standing line and free end to snug up the knot.

Attaching Lure to Line—Mono: Loop Knot

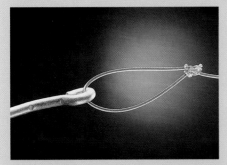

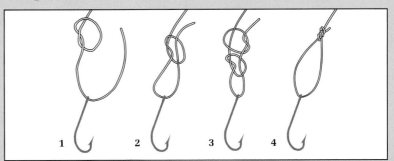

*A **loop knot** allows your lure to swing more freely, so it has better action than a lure that is snubbed down tightly.*

(1) Make an overhand knot near the end of the line and put the free end through the lure eye; (2) pass the free end through the overhand knot; (3) with the free end, make an overhand knot around the standing line (where you tie the second overhand determines the size of the loop); (4) tighten the overhand knots and pull the standing line to snug up the knot.

Splicing Lines of Similar Diameter—Mono: Blood Knot

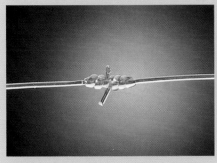

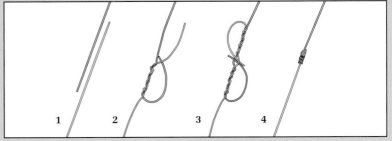

*A **blood knot** looks complex, but is quite simple to tie. Don't try it with lines of greatly different diameters or different materials.*

(1) Hold the lines alongside each other, with the ends facing opposite directions; (2) wrap one line around the other 4-5 times, and pass the free end between the two lines, as shown; (3) repeat step 2 with the other line; (4) pull on both lines to snug up the knot.

Splicing Mono of Different Diameter or Mono to Superline: Double Uni-Knot

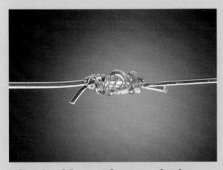

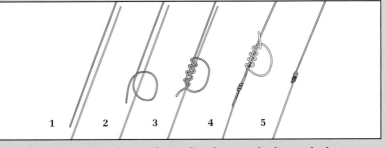

*The **double uni-knot** is the best way to splice mono to superline. It works well for any lines of different material or diameter.*

(1) Hold the lines alongside each other, with the ends facing opposite directions; (2) form a loop with one of the lines, as shown; (3) pass the free end through the loop and around the standing line 4-5 times and then snug up the knot; (4) repeat steps 2 and 3 with the other line; (5) pull on both lines to draw the two knots together.

Most serious bass anglers use a compartmentalized tackle-storage system. Rather than cramming all their lures into one big tackle box, they carry individual boxes for each important type of lure. These boxes are labeled and carried in either a hard-sided box (left) or a soft pack (right).

ACCESSORIES

Open any bass-fishing catalog and you'll see page after page of gadgets intended to help put more bass in your boat. Some of these devices will, in fact, improve your fishing success, but you can easily live without most of them. Here are the items you're most likely to need:

• **Polarized Sunglasses.** Not only will polarized sunglasses help protect your eyes from bright sunlight, they remove the glare from the

Polarized sunglasses enable you to clearly see fish in shallow water (left). Without the glasses, you may see vague shadows but not definite shapes (right) because of glare.

water so you can see what's beneath the surface.

• **Needlenose Pliers.** A pair of needlenose pliers comes in handy for straightening bent hooks and quickly removing hooks so bass can be released unharmed.

• **Hook Sharpener.** The hooks on most out-of-the-package lures are surprisingly dull. Before you use these lures, touch up the hooks with a file or hook hone to give them a needle-sharp point.

• **Line Cutter.** An ordinary fingernail clipper is all you need for cutting monofilament. For superline, however, you'll need a pair of extra-sharp scissors.

• **Tool Kit.** Always carry a tool kit for making on-the-water repairs to your boat and motor. The kit should contain a set of screwdrivers, open-end wrenches and socket wrenches, including a spark-

It takes a tiny screwdriver to tighten small reel screws.

plug wrench. Carry some replacement spark plugs, fuses and electrical connectors as well.

For repairing fishing reels and other small tackle items, you'll need a set of tiny screwdrivers, including both standard and Phillips.

• **Marker Buoys.** When you want to pinpoint a school of bass or a specific structural element, simply toss out a marker buoy. For convenience, buy a set of markers that fit into a handy storage rack.

• **Plug Knocker.** Designed to dislodge snagged lures, these devices clip onto your line and slide down on a separate cord to knock the bait off the obstruction.

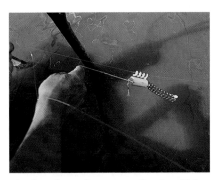

A plug knocker pays for itself in a hurry by freeing expensive lures.

• **Brush Clamp.** When fishing in brushy cover, you can secure your boat with a metal clip, called a brush clamp, rather than dropping anchor and spooking the fish.

• **Logbook.** Recording your daily catch, including water temperature, depth, weather

The seconds it takes to fill in a logbook can save hours of future exploration.

conditions, time of day and lure selection, can be a big help in quickly finding the pattern on a later date.

• **Electronic Scale.** These battery-powered, digital scales give you a precise weight of fish you release. Some are accurate to within one ounce.

• **Camera.** Carry a small, water-resistant camera in your boat to furnish "evidence" on fish you release.

• **Flashlight.** It's a good idea to carry a flashlight, not only for fishing after dark but for replacing a fuse or making other repairs in a dark corner of your boat.

• **Cell Phone.** A cell phone can save the day should you damage your prop, experience engine failure or have any other kind of problem far from the boat landing.

A brush clamp makes it easy to secure your boat.

LURES, BAITS AND HOW TO USE THEM

*L*earning when, where and how to use a wide variety of lures and baits is the key to consistent bass-fishing success.

LURE SELECTION

No other freshwater game-fish will strike as many different artificial lures as the largemouth bass. In fact, it would be difficult to find a bait a bass *won't* strike.

The challenge for the bass angler, then, is to find the lure or bait that best suits the conditions and the activity level of the fish.

If you had unlimited time, you could keep trying different offerings until you found what the bass want. But you can find the answer much faster and easier by making your selection based on the following considerations:

Type of Cover

When you're fishing on a clean bottom, your lure choices are endless. But bass are cover-oriented, so that is seldom the case. Chances are, you'll find them in or around submerged weeds, brush, timber, rocks, docks, floating-leaved weeds or weed mats.

The type and density of the cover dictates what lures you can and can't use. Some weeds, such as broadleaf cabbage, have crispy leaves that shatter when an open-hooked lure is ripped through them. But most weeds are tough or stringy; instead of shattering, they catch on the nose of your lure or foul your hooks.

You could rip a crankbait through a sparse stand of cabbage, but in a dense stand of

cabbage or a bed of stringy weeds such as milfoil or hydrilla, you'll do better with a lure that has a protected hook, such as a Texas-rigged plastic worm. To fish a heavy weed mat, especially one with lots of filamentous algae, try working a weedless frog or rat over the surface. To get under a dock or other over-hanging cover, skip-cast (p. 95) with a lightly weighted soft plastic, such as a tube-bait, which has a large enough diameter that it will skip off the surface.

Depth

Once you determine the depth where the majority of the bass are holding, you need to select a lure that runs at that level or just above it. Remember that the fish are more likely to come up for a lure than go down for one.

Some lures, such as crankbaits, are designed to run at a specific depth. Others, like jigs, spinnerbaits and sinking minnowbaits, can be fished over a wide depth range by varying your retrieve.

It pays to take some time and experiment with a variety of lures to determine which ones would be good choices when you find fish at a particular depth range.

Activity Level of Fish

Bass get progressively more active (and feed more heavily) as the water gets warmer. Beyond 80°F, however, their activity level begins to decrease. Weather-related factors, like cold fronts and thunderstorms, also influence their activity level.

As a rule, as bass get more active, they prefer faster-

Bass in clear water go for the natural look.

moving lures and those with a more intense action. While the subtle wiggle of a slowly retrieved minnowbait may be the ticket in early spring, a faster retrieve with a wide-wobbling crankbait is more likely to draw a strike in the heat of summer.

Type of Forage

In bass fishing, there is sel-dom a need to "match the hatch." However, there are times when bass key in on forage of a particular size. When there is a huge supply of young-of-the-year gizzard shad, for example, you'll gen-erally have best results on a lure that is the approximate size and shape of the shad.

This explains why savvy anglers often use large baits in spring, before any young-of-the-year baitfish have hatched; switch to smaller baits in early summer, when

young baitfish become avail-able; and then progress to larger baits in fall to keep up with baitfish growth.

Water Clarity

Water clarity is a consider-ation not only in the type of lure you select, but in the color.

In a murky lake where the visibility is only a few inches, a bait that emits a lot of noise or vibration, such as a rattle-bait or spinnerbait, is usually the best choice. Even if the bass can't see it, they can hear it or detect it with their lateral-line sense.

In clear water, where bass can get a good look at the bait, dark, drab or natural col-ors usually outproduce bright, gaudy or fluorescent colors. In low clarity water, the reverse is generally true.

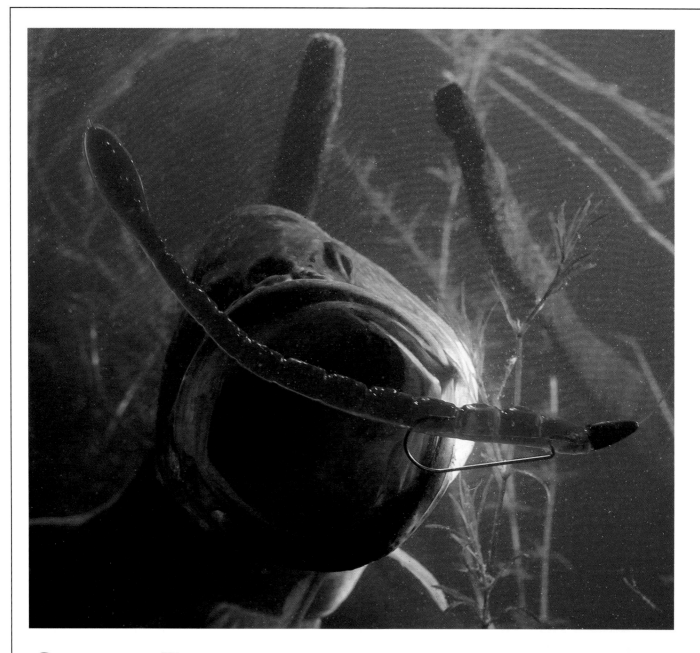

SOFT PLASTICS

It's not surprising that soft-plastic lures enjoy tremendous popularity among largemouth anglers. Soft plastics have a remarkably lifelike texture, so bass pick them up and hold onto them longer than they would any other kind of artificial lure.

The pliable material gives bass anglers another important edge. Rigged "Texas-style" (with the hook point buried in the plastic), the lures are virtually weedless. Yet a sharp hookset will push the point through the plastic and into the fish's jaw.

On the pages that follow are tips for selecting and fishing with each type of soft-plastic lure popular among bass anglers. Grubs and other soft plastics normally used to tip jigs will be discussed in "Lead-Head Jigs" (pp. 114-119).

Recommended Tackle

A 6-foot, medium-power spinning outfit with 6- to 8-pound-test mono is adequate for fishing most soft plastics up to 4 inches in length. For larger baits, you'll need a medium-heavy-power, fast-action baitcasting outfit from 6 to 6½ feet long with 12- to 20-pound mono. When Texas-rigging (pp. 90-91), you'll need a stiff rod to drive the hook through the plastic.

PLASTIC WORMS

You'll find plastic worms in the tackle box of every serious largemouth angler. Worms catch bass in cold water as well as warm, you can snake them through the thickest cover and, to the bass, they feel like real food. Most anglers view plastic worms as a good choice for weedy, brushy or snaggy cover, although worms are effective on a clean bottom as well.

But worms are usually retrieved slowly, so they do not make good "locator" lures. When you're searching for bass, it's better to use a crankbait, spinnerbait or other lure that covers water in a hurry. Once you find the fish, you can switch to a worm to cover the area more thoroughly and tempt non-aggressive feeders.

Here are the main considerations in selecting plastic worms:

• **Size.** Most largemouth anglers use worms in the 6- to 8-inch range, but when the fish are finicky, you may want to try finesse fishing (p. 95) with a small bait, such as a 4-inch "Weinee" worm. Anglers fishing for giant Florida bass use worms up to 16 inches long.

• **Type of Tail.** Worms are available in curlytail, augertail, paddletail and straight-tail models. Curlytails and augertails have the most action and are usually the best choice in discolored water, because the tails emit an intense vibration that bass can detect with their lateral-line sense. Paddletails have a slow-

er throbbing action and straight-tails have virtually no action, other than that which the angler imparts. It pays to carry a selection of all four styles in a variety of colors. Experiment to find what works best on a given day.

• **Buoyancy.** Most plastic worms are slightly buoyant, but a heavy worm hook will sink them. If you want to fish your worm on the surface or float it up on a Carolina rig (p. 90), you'll need a worm with extra buoyancy. Some highly buoyant worms have air bubbles impregnated into the plastic.

• **Hardness.** For Texas-rigging, always use a soft-bodied worm so the hook point can easily penetrate the plastic on

the hookset. Soft-bodied worms also have more tail action and feel more lifelike. But worms made from harder plastic are more durable and last longer. They work well for fishing on a clean bottom where you don't have to bury the hook, and are preferable on pre-rigged worms.

• **Scent/Taste.** Some anglers swear by scent-impregnated or salt-coated worms. They maintain that bass hold onto these baits longer, giving them time to set the hook. But others say scent and taste make little difference. Draw your own conclusions.

Types of Plastic Worms

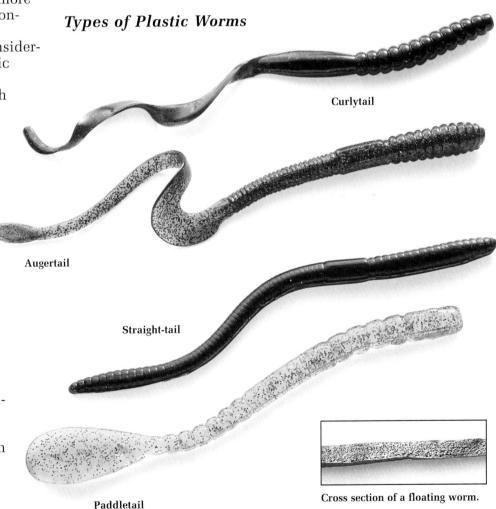

Curlytail

Augertail

Straight-tail

Paddletail

Cross section of a floating worm.

Rigging Plastic Worms

How you rig a plastic worm depends mainly on the type of cover you'll be fishing. In dense weeds or brush, worms should be Texas-rigged so the hook point is protected.

But in very heavy cover, your weight could easily separate from your worm, so you'll have trouble feeling a take. To solve the problem, use a Florida rig or peg the sinker to the line with a piece of toothpick (p. 95).

The main drawback to Texas-rigging is that the weight carries the worm to the bottom where weeds or other cover may prevent fish from seeing it. In this situation, a Carolina rig is a better choice. Because the worm is separated from the weight, it floats up high enough for fish to get a good look at it.

You can also fish a worm on a split-shot rig or mushroom head jig (p. 118).

Hooks commonly used for rigging worms are shown at right. For a 4-inch worm, use a #1 or 2 hook; a 6-inch, 2/0 or 3/0; an 8-inch, 4/0 or 5/0 and a 10-inch, 5/0 or 6/0.

Common Worm Hooks

Mister Twister Keeper Hook

Tru-Turn EZ Link

Shaw Grigsby HP Hook

Blue Fox Hidden Head Worm Hook

Tru-Turn Cam Action

Straight Worm Hook

Offset Hook

How to Rig Plastic Worms

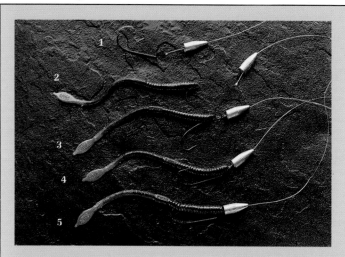

Texas Rig. (1) Thread a bullet sinker onto your line and tie on a worm hook. **(2)** Insert the point of the hook into the head, push it in about $1/2$ inch and bring it out the side. **(3)** Push the hook all the way through the bait so only the hook eye protrudes at the head. **(4)** Rotate the hook 180 degrees. **(5)** Push the hook into the bait; the hook point should almost come out the other side and the bait should hang straight.

Carolina Rig. Thread a $1/4$- to 1-ounce bullet sinker and a glass or plastic bead onto your line and attach a barrel swivel. Tie on an 18- to 36-inch leader of lighter mono and attach a worm hook. Push the hook into a buoyant worm and out the side, leaving the point exposed.

Florida Rig. Thread a screw-in weight (inset) onto your line and attach a worm hook. Then screw the sinker into the head of the bait. This way, the weight won't separate from the bait when you hang up on a branch or other obstacle.

1 Make a cast and then hold the rod tip at about 1 o'clock as the bait starts to sink. Keep your line slightly taut, but not tight. The fish often grab the worm when it's sinking and if your line is not taut, you won't feel the take.

2 Gradually lower your rod tip, keeping your line slightly taut as the bait continues to sink. By the time the bait hits bottom, your rod tip should be at the 3 o'clock position. If you kept your rod tip high, it would be hard to set the hook.

3 Continue retrieving with a lift-and-drop motion. When you feel a take or your line starts moving off to the side, drop your rod tip to reduce the tension. If the fish feels too much resistance, it will drop the lure.

4 Set the hook with a powerful upward snap of your wrists and forearms. A strong hookset is necessary to drive the hook through the worm and into the fish's jaw.

How to Fish a Carolina-Rigged Worm

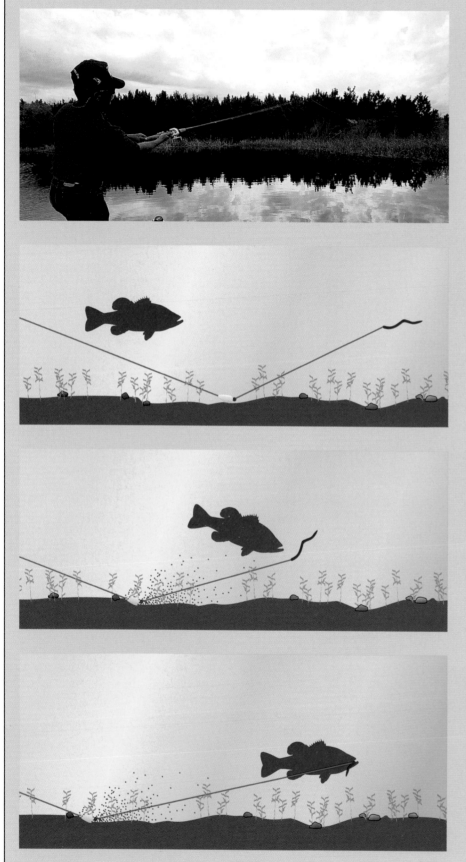

1 Using a long-handled baitcasting rod, make a sidearm lob-cast. If you try tossing a Carolina rig with an overhand snap-cast, it will probably tangle.

2 After the sinker hits bottom, begin a slow, steady retrieve. A rapid retrieve will pull the lure down so far that the fish may not see it.

3 Give the rig a periodic jerk to change the action. The worm will dip down and then slowly float back up and the sinker will kick up a cloud of silt. The sudden change often draws a fish's attention and triggers a strike.

4 When you feel a pick-up or any kind of resistance, drop your rod tip and hesitate a second or two to make sure the fish has the hook in its mouth. The line can slip through the sinker, so the fish will feel no resistance. Set the hook with a firm upward snap of the wrists.

PLASTIC LIZARDS & CRAWS

Lizards and craws are rigged and fished in much the same way as plastic worms, but there will be times when they'll catch more bass. The wiggling legs or pincers give the baits an enticing action and make them sink more slowly than most worms. Craws and small lizards can also be used for tipping jigs (p. 116).

Because crayfish are one of the largemouth's favorite foods, the effectiveness of plastic craws should come as no surprise. Although bass seldom encounter real lizards, they may feed on larval salamanders, which have a lizard-like shape. Plastic lizards work especially well at spawning time, probably because larval salamanders are a threat to largemouth nests. When one gets too close to the spawning bed, the bass picks it up and removes it.

Lizards used for largemouth are generally 6 to 9 inches long, although specialty lizards used for big Florida bass may be as long as 15 inches.

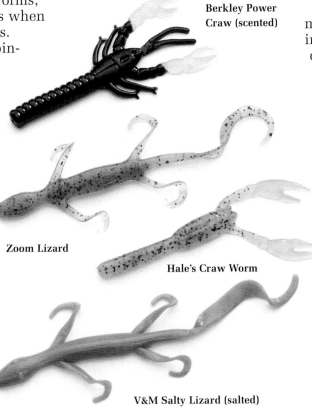

Berkley Power Craw (scented)

Zoom Lizard

Hale's Craw Worm

V&M Salty Lizard (salted)

TUBEBAITS

These hollow-bodied, 4- to 6-inch baits have tentacles at the rear that give the lure a unique action. By rapidly shaking the rod tip, you can make the tentacles quiver enticingly while barely moving the bait.

This ultrarealistic action explains why tubebaits are considered one of the top lures for sight-fishing fussy clearwater bass.

How to Rig a Tubebait

Bullet-Sinker Method.
Thread on a bullet sinker and tie on an Eagle Claw HP hook. Push the hook through the nose of the bait and out the side (left). Give the hook a half turn, push it through

until only the eye protrudes, and then attach the wire clip to the shank (middle). Push the hook through the tube so the point just barely starts to penetrate the opposite side (right).

Internal-Weight Method. *Drop a specially designed weight down the inside of the tube so the ring rests at the head of the bait (left). Next, push the hook point into the head of the bait and through the ring (middle). Then, continue rigging as in the sequence above until the lure is completely rigged (right). A*

Soft Jerkbaits

These slow-sinking baits, also called "soft stickbaits" or "slugs," have a wounded-baitfish action intended to draw strikes from finicky bass. They're commonly used during the post-spawn period, when the fish turn up their noses at most lures.

Because soft jerkbaits sink so slowly, they work best when bass are in the shallows. They are normally rigged with little or no weight, so they're hard to fish in windy

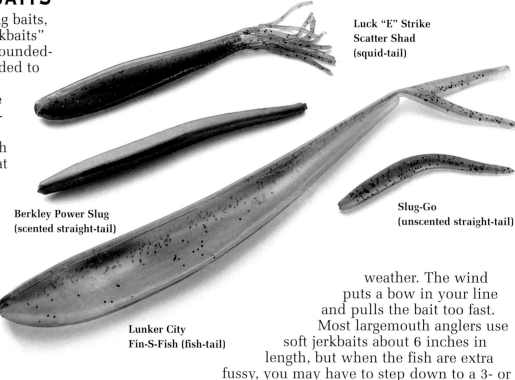

Luck "E" Strike Scatter Shad (squid-tail)

Berkley Power Slug (scented straight-tail)

Slug-Go (unscented straight-tail)

Lunker City Fin-S-Fish (fish-tail)

weather. The wind puts a bow in your line and pulls the bait too fast. Most largemouth anglers use soft jerkbaits about 6 inches in length, but when the fish are extra fussy, you may have to step down to a 3- or 4-incher. Anglers seeking trophy bass may use soft jerkbaits up to 10 inches long.

Retrieve a soft jerkbait with a series of gentle downward pulls to make the lure glide from side to side in a horizontal attitude.

How to Rig a Soft Jerkbait

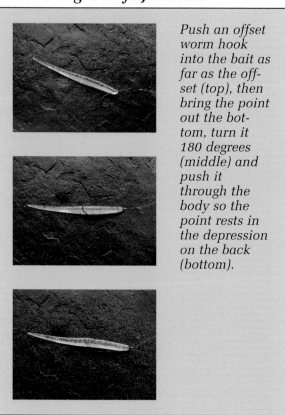

Push an offset worm hook into the bait as far as the offset (top), then bring the point out the bottom, turn it 180 degrees (middle) and push it through the body so the point rests in the depression on the back (bottom).

Tips for Fishing with Soft Plastics

Skip a bulky worm under a dock or other over-head cover by making a sidearm cast with a spinning outfit. Slim-bodied worms do not have enough surface area to skip well.

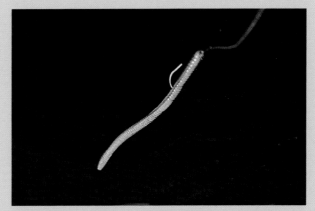

Fish a floating worm on the surface to catch largemouth in shallow water. Twitch the bait on a slack line to give it an erratic side-to-side action without moving forward too fast.

Peg the bullet sinker onto the line so it won't separate from the bait in heavy cover. Just wedge a toothpick into the hole in the sinker and then break off the end.

Thread on a brass sinker and one or two glass beads before tying on your worm hook. The sharp clinking sound made by the "brass 'n' glass" makes it easier for bass to locate the bait.

Make a soft stickbait run deeper by pushing a lead insert or finishing nail into the plastic just ahead of the hook bend. An insert also helps you make longer casts and keeps the wind from moving the bait too fast.

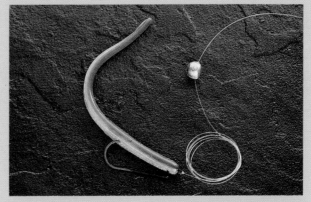

To tempt fussy bass, try "finesse fishing" with a light spinning outfit and a small soft plastic on a split-shot rig. "Stitch" in line with your fingers; this way, the rig will creep along slowly enough to keep the bait floating above the bottom.

SPINNERBAITS & SPINNERS

The flash and vibration produced by a whirling spinner blade are a combination that largemouth bass find hard to resist. Bass anglers use two kinds of spinner-type lures: spinnerbaits and in-line spinners.

SPINNERBAITS

These versatile lures are ideal in many common bass-fishing situations. You can run them through dense weeds, bump them across a brush pile, bulge them on the surface, helicopter them alongside vertical cover and even jig them along the bottom.

Types of Spinnerbaits

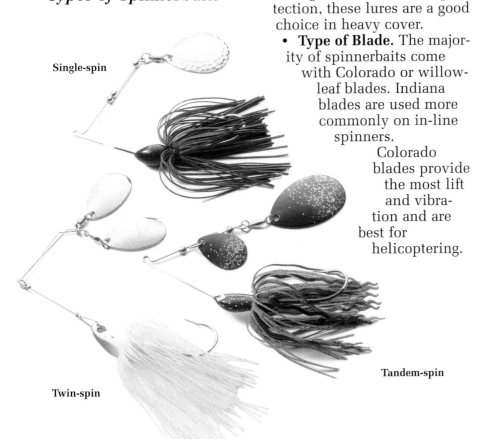

Single-spin

Twin-spin

Tandem-spin

Not only do spinnerbaits have a special appeal to largemouth, they are almost completely weedless because the safety-pin shaft runs interference for the blade and upturned hook.

Here are the main things to look for in a spinnerbait:
- **Blade Configuration.** A *single-spin* has just one spinner blade attached to the upper arm. Single-spins produce a strong beat and work well for helicoptering (p. 99).

A *tandem-spin* has two blades on the upper arm for extra "lift." It will generally run shallower than a single spin at the same retrieve speed.

A *twin-spin* has a pair of upper arms, each with a single blade. Because the twin arms give the hook more protection, these lures are a good choice in heavy cover.
- **Type of Blade.** The majority of spinnerbaits come with Colorado or willow-leaf blades. Indiana blades are used more commonly on in-line spinners.

Colorado blades provide the most lift and vibration and are best for helicoptering.

Types of Spinner Blades

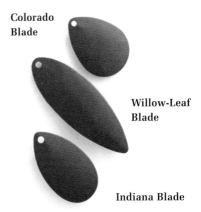

Colorado Blade

Willow-Leaf Blade

Indiana Blade

Willow-leaf blades have much less lift and vibration, but produce a lot of flash. Indiana blades have intermediate qualities.
- **Type of Skirt.** The rippling skirt of a spinnerbait greatly adds to the lure's appeal. Spinnerbait skirts are usually made of live-rubber or silicone, although a few have hair, feather, vinyl, tinsel or mylar skirts.

Silicone skirts work well in clear water, because the clear or translucent material has a lifelike look. Live-rubber skirts are a better choice in discolored water, because they produce more vibration.

For even more attraction, many anglers tip their spinnerbait with some type of pork or soft-plastic trailer. A bulky trailer also adds buoyancy, so you can easily keep the lure above the weed tops.
- **Weight.** The weight of your spinnerbait depends mainly on the water depth. A ¼-ounce bait will do the job at a depth of 10 feet or less, but some anglers use spinnerbaits weighing as much as 1 ounce to fish depths of 20 feet or more.

How to Fish a Spinnerbait

It's hard to fish a spinnerbait the wrong way. All you really have to do is cast it out and reel it in just fast enough to keep the blades turning. But it pays to know the variations on the basic retrieve shown in these pages.

Once you're comfortable with these different retrieves, you can combine them to cover the water more thoroughly. For example, you could bulge the lure over a weed flat, let it helicopter down a drop-off at the edge of the weeds and then slow-roll it along the bottom in deep water.

Whenever possible, bump your spinnerbait into a stick-up or some other type of cover on the retrieve. Any interruption in the beat of the blade will draw attention to the lure and trigger strikes.

Although largemouth often attack a spinnerbait aggressively, there will be times when strikes are hard to detect. You may feel nothing more than a slight hesitation in the beat of the blade. If you feel anything unusual, set the hook immediately.

Spinnerbait Retrieve Variations

Stop-and-Go. Instead of reeling steadily, pause periodically and allow the bait to flutter down; then, resume reeling. This erratic retrieve causes the beat of the blade to change, often triggering more strikes than a steady retrieve.
Experiment with the duration of the pauses until you find the tempo that works best.

Slow-Rolling. Reel just fast enough, so the blades barely turn, while allowing the lure to bump along the bottom or crawl over obstacles such as logs or rock piles.

Spinnerbaiting Tips

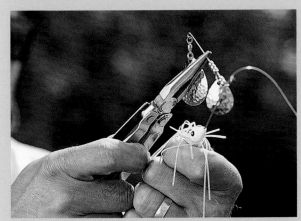

Tune a spinnerbait by aligning the upper shaft with the lower. If the shafts are out of line, the lure will tip to the side on the retrieve.

To improve your hooking percentage, use a spinnerbait with a titanium shaft that is flexible enough to bend inward when a fish strikes. A titanium shaft also transmits vibrations well, can be bent repeatedly without weakening and will always spring back to the same shape.

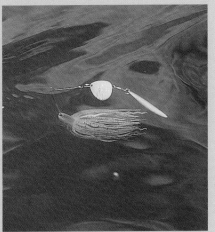

Bulging. Keep your rod tip high and reel just fast enough so the blades make a bulge in the surface. Or, reel even faster and make the blades break water.

Helicoptering. Cast a spinnerbait to vertical cover, such as a rock ledge or flooded tree and then feed line as the lure sinks. The helicoptering blade slows the sink rate and draws the attention of bass.

react quickly, darting out to grab it before the current carries it away. The flash of a spinner blade catches their eye and triggers a quick reaction strike.

Another reason spinners work so well in current is that the moving water causes the blade to spin. So you can retrieve very slowly and the blade still turns rapidly, producing not only flash but lots of vibration.

Lake fishermen use in-line spinners to work shallow cover such as rocky points and gravelly shoals. You can also run an in-line spinner over shallow weed tops or count it down to fish deeper structure.

Largemouth anglers use two basic types of in-line spinners:

• **French Spinner.** These lures emit intense vibrations, so they work especially well in discolored water.

A French spinner has a blade that rotates around the shaft on a metal attachment device called a *clevis*. Behind the blade is a weighted body and a treble hook, which may be dressed with feathers or a soft-plastic body.

• **Sonic Spinner.** Because of the "sonic" blade's unique design (convex on one end and concave on the other), it catches a lot of water and spins easily even in slow current. But the blade spins directly on the shaft, rather than on a clevis, so the lure produces less vibrations than a French spinner.

The secret to catching bass on an in-line spinner is find-

In-Line Spinners

When asked to name their favorite largemouth lures, few bass pros would include in-line spinners because they can't be fished in heavy cover. Weeds will catch on the open hooks and foul the blade, preventing it from turning. But

in-line spinners are still very popular among certain factions of bass anglers, particularly stream fishermen.

Stream-dwelling largemouth spend most of their time lying behind a boulder, log or other object that provides shelter from the current. When these bass spot a food item, they

Some Popular In-Line Spinners

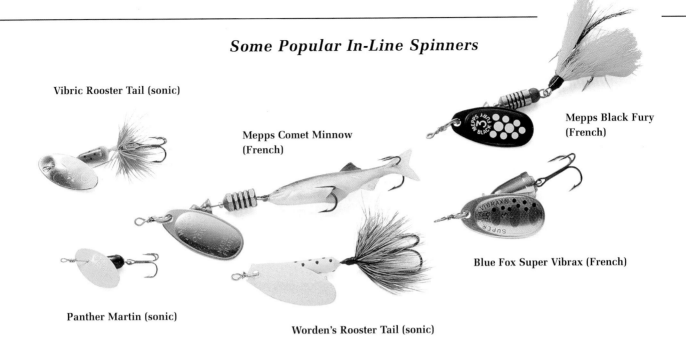

Vibric Rooster Tail (sonic)

Mepps Comet Minnow (French)

Mepps Black Fury (French)

Blue Fox Super Vibrax (French)

Panther Martin (sonic)

Worden's Rooster Tail (sonic)

ing the right retrieve speed. If you reel too fast, the lure will lose depth; too slow, and it will sink to the bottom and snag or foul. As a rule, you want to keep the bait just off the bottom with the blade turning steadily.

The biggest problem in fishing an in-line spinner is line twist. Always attach the lure with a snap-swivel, or bend the main shaft (right) so the lure can't spin.

In-line spinners used for largemouth usually weigh ½ ounce or less and have a size 2 to 5 blade.

Spinner-Fishing Tips

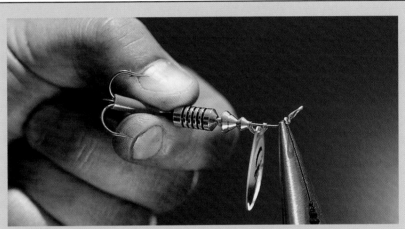

To eliminate line twist, bend the shaft of an in-line spinner upward at about a 45-degree angle. This way, you will not have to attach a bulky snap-swivel.

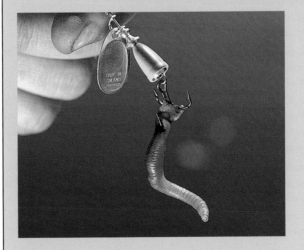

For extra attraction, tip an in-line spinner with live bait such as a minnow, leech or piece of nightcrawler.

Recommended Tackle

A 6- to 6½-foot, medium-power spinning rod with a fairly soft tip is ideal for casting in-line spinners. The soft tip allows the rod to "load" from the weight of the light lure, so you can cast more accurately and with less effort. Pair the rod with a wide-spool spinning reel filled with 6- to 8-pound-test mono.

TOPWATERS

When you see the water explode as a largemouth inhales a surface lure, it's easy to understand why topwater fishing gets in your blood.

But the excitement itself doesn't explain why so many accomplished largemouth anglers rely on topwaters.

There are times when they will outproduce any other kind of bass lure. As a rule, topwaters do not work well at water temperatures below 60°F.

The topwater lures shown on these pages are intended solely for fishing on the surface. Some other lures, such as floating minnowbaits, can also be used as topwaters, but they are not included here because they are used for subsurface presentations as well.

The topwater lures most commonly used in largemouth fishing include:

STICKBAITS

These long, thin plugs are weighted in the tail, so they float with their head up (right). When retrieved with a series of downward strokes of the rod, the lure will veer from side to side. This enticing retrieve is called "walking the dog."

Because stickbaits make less commotion than most other topwaters, their appeal is mainly visual. They work

best in water that is relatively clear and calm.

How to "Walk the Dog"

To walk the dog, point your rod directly at the lure, give it a sharp downward stroke and then stop the rod at about 5 o'clock (left). Immediately after completing the downward stroke, lift your rod to throw slack into the line. This way, your lure will dart sharply to one side (top right). After the lure completes its sideways glide, give it another sharp downward stroke and throw slack into the line to make it dart in the opposite direction (bottom right).

PROPBAITS

With propellers at one or both ends, these lures have a sputtering action that attracts bass even under low-visibility conditions. Some models have a lip for extra action. Propbaits are an excellent choice for fishing in muddy or choppy water or at night.

Propbaits can be fished with a slow, steady retrieve, but they normally work better with a twitch-and-pause retrieve. Try varying the length of your twitches and the duration of your pauses until you find the right combination. By twitching the lure sharply on a slack line, you can make the blades throw water while barely moving the lure.

Because propbaits have no tail weight, they cannot be fished with a walk-the-dog retrieve.

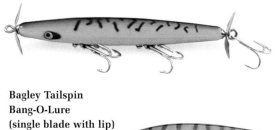

Smithwick Devil's Horse (twin blade)

Bagley Tailspin Bang-O-Lure (single blade with lip)

Arbogast Snooker (single blade)

CRAWLERS

The enticing gurgle of a crawler has long been and still is irresistible to largemouth bass. The crawling action and gurgling sound is produced by a wide faceplate or a pair of "arms" on the side of the lure.

Crawlers can be retrieved quite rapidly, so they work well for locating fish. And because they're so noisy, they'll catch bass even at night or in discolored water. Arm-type crawlers are not a good choice in dense weeds because the arms tend to collect sprigs of vegetation.

A steady retrieve will normally draw the most strikes, but you'll have to experiment with the speed of your retrieve. If it's too fast, the lure will skip on the surface and lose action; too slow, and the lure won't crawl properly or produce the gurgling sound. If a steady retrieve is not working, however, try a twitch-and-pause retrieve.

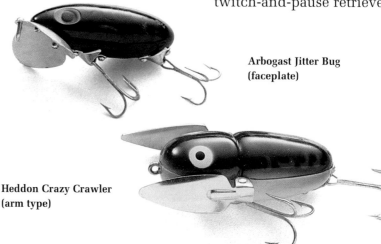

Arbogast Jitter Bug (faceplate)

Heddon Crazy Crawler (arm type)

CHUGGERS

These lures make a chugging or popping sound and throw water when you retrieve them with sharp twitches. The action resembles that of a kicking frog, explaining why the lures are so effective for largemouth bass.

Chuggers, often called poppers, are commonly retrieved with a series of non-stop twitches. This rapid chugging retrieve enables you to cover a lot of water in a short time and appeals to actively feeding bass.

But you can also work a chugger with twitches followed by pauses. Try varying the length of the pauses until you find what works best. Sometimes, a pause of a few seconds is all that's necessary. Other times, you may have to wait for all the ripples to sub-

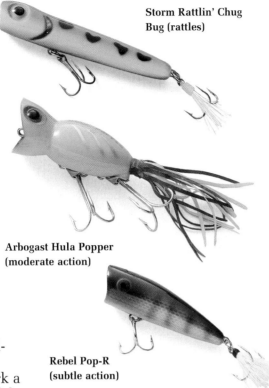

Storm Rattlin' Chug Bug (rattles)

Arbogast Hula Popper (moderate action)

Rebel Pop-R (subtle action)

side, which can take nearly a minute.

There will be times when the fish prefer a fair amount of splash and other times when they want practically none. How much commotion

a chugger makes depends on its design and how hard you twitch it. Chuggers with a flattened face do not catch as much water as those with a grooved or dished-out face, so they generally have a more subtle action.

In most cases, light to moderate twitches will do the job. Violent splashes are more likely to spook largemouth than entice them to strike.

Recommended Tackle

A 6½-foot medium-power, medium-action baitcasting rod is a good choice for fishing chuggers because it flexes enough to allow pinpoint casting with these lures, many of which are relatively light. Pair this with a narrow-spool, high-speed baitcasting reel, which enables you to make a rapid twitching retrieve. Spool up with 12- to 20-pound-test mono. Tie the lure directly to your line.

How to "Chug" a Chugger

Make a cast and then start retrieving with rapid twitches while holding your rod at about 2 o'clock. Keeping your rod tip high prevents the line from sinking.

As the lure approaches the boat, keep twitching while gradually lowering the rod to about 5 o'clock. If you keep the rod too high, you'll lift the face of the bait so much that it won't throw water.

FROGS & RATS

Topwater frogs and rats are ideal for drawing bass out of dense cover. They work well for covering expanses of matted weeds, such as hydrilla or milfoil and are one of the few lures that can be fished in "slop," an impenetrable mixture of matted weeds and filamentous algae.

Frogs and rats work best in hot weather, because that's when bass seek out cool, shaded areas under the matted weeds.

Because frogs and rats have light foam rubber or hollow-plastic bodies, they slide over the vegetation rather than sink into it. Most have a weedguard or upturned hooks that won't foul in the vegetation.

The pliable body makes these lures feel like real food, so a bass is likely to hold onto them longer than it would a hard bait. Some frogs have lifelike legs that add even more realism.

Harrison Hoge Superfrog

Phelps Marsh Mouse

Recommended Tackle

Frogs and rats are normally fished in heavy cover, so they require heavy tackle. A 7½-foot flippin' stick and a baitcasting reel spooled with 20- to 30-pound abrasion-resistant mono or superline makes a perfect setup. Always tie frogs and rats directly to the line.

Tips for Fishing Frogs & Rats

Slide a frog or rat over matted weeds and into an open pocket. Hesitate for a few seconds to let the ripples subside. That's when a bass usually strikes.

Give a frog a sharp twitch to make the legs kick. Be sure to twitch on a slack line so the lure doesn't scoot ahead too far.

BUZZBAITS

A buzzbait is one of the best lures for locating bass because you can cast it a long distance and retrieve it rapidly, covering a lot of water in a short time. Although a buzzbait may draw strikes from only a small percentage of the fish (the active feeders), you can switch to a

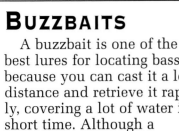

Norman Triple Wing Buzzbait (safety-pin)

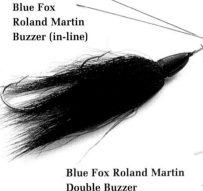

Blue Fox Roland Martin Buzzer (in-line)

Blue Fox Roland Martin Double Buzzer (safety-pin double-blade)

slower presentation once you have them pinpointed.

Buzzbaits have one or two large blades on either a straight-wire or safety-pin shaft, so they produce an intense gurgling action and throw a lot of water. This explains why they work well even in choppy or discolored water, or at night.

A safety-pin buzzer is the best choice in weedy or brushy cover, because the shaft prevents the upturned hook from fouling or hanging up.

In-line buzzers work better in snag-free cover. The exposed hook (either single or treble) will improve your hooking percentage.

Like other topwaters, buzzbaits should be tied directly to the line. A heavy leader or clip will sink the nose, preventing the blade from spinning.

Recommended Tackle

A fast-action, 7½-foot flippin' stick works well for buzzbait fishing, because it enables you to make long casts and keep your rod tip high at the start of the retrieve. You'll need a high-speed baitcasting reel (gear-ratio of at least 6:1) for rapid retrieves. Spool up with 17- to 20-pound-test mono.

Buzzbaiting Tips

Keep your rod tip high at the beginning of the retrieve. This lifts the nose of the bait so the blade can spin freely. Gradually lower your rod as the lure approaches the boat.

To retrieve a buzzbait more slowly, try cupping the blades so they catch more water. Otherwise, they may not spin on a slow retrieve.

SUBSURFACE PLUGS

When you need to cover a lot of water to locate bass, there is no better choice than a subsurface plug. Not only can you retrieve these baits rapidly, they emit a vibration that attracts bass from a distance.

As a rule, subsurface plugs work best at water temperatures of 50°F or higher but, if you slow down your retrieve, they'll catch bass when the water is much colder.

Because subsurface plugs have exposed hooks, they are not the best choice in dense weedy or woody cover. However, you can easily fish them along a weedline or run them over the weedtops to draw fish out of the vegeta-tion. And you can rip them through certain types of sparse weeds.

Most bass plugs are 3 to 5 inches in length although a few plugs, used mainly for giant Florida bass, are more than a foot long.

Here are the most popular types of subsurface plugs used for largemouth:

CRANKBAITS

A crankbait has a plastic or metal lip that gives the lure a side-to-side wiggling or wobbling action and causes it to dive. How deep it dives depends mainly on the size, shape and angle of the lip. As a rule, the larger the lip and the straighter its angle in relation to the plug's horizontal axis, the deeper the lure will dive. Plugs with a narrow lip have a tight wiggle; those with a broad lip, a greater side-to-side wobble.

Body shape also affects a crankbait's action and stability. As a rule, the thinner the body, the tighter and faster the wobble.

Although most crankbaits float, some have internal lead weights to make them sink or suspend. A bait that sinks can be counted down to reach fish at any depth; one that suspends can be fished very slowly yet will not float up like a normal crankbait.

An erratic crankbait retrieve usually triggers more strikes than a steady one. Try to make the lure bump bottom or some type of cover to interrupt its action. If there is no cover to alter the action, try a stop-and-go retrieve.

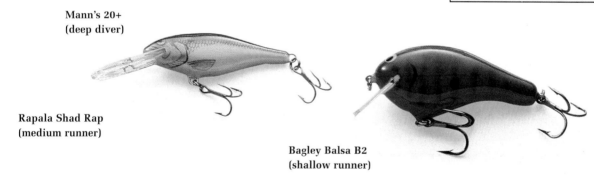

Mann's 20+
(deep diver)

Rapala Shad Rap
(medium runner)

Bagley Balsa B2
(shallow runner)

Recommended Tackle

Lengthy casts are important in crankbait fishing, so it pays to use a baitcasting rod from 6½ to 7½ feet long, for extra casting leverage. Many anglers prefer a rod with a soft tip, which allows the fish to take the bait farther into its mouth before the hookset. Use a high-gear-ratio (at least 5:1) reel and spool it with 14- to 25-pound-test mono. If the plug has a split ring, tie it directly to your line. Otherwise, use a round-nosed snap.

Crankbaiting Tips

Tune a crankbait if it is running to the side. Otherwise it will not reach its maximum depth. Bend the attachment eye in the direction opposite to that in which the lure is tracking. If it's tracking to the left, for example, bend the eye to the right and then test the action.

Bump your crankbait off rocks, logs or other obstructions; the change of action often triggers a strike.

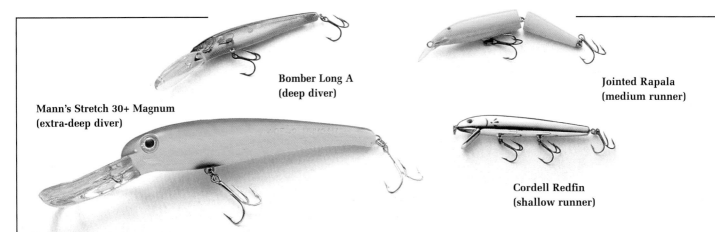

Mann's Stretch 30+ Magnum
(extra-deep diver)

Bomber Long A
(deep diver)

Jointed Rapala
(medium runner)

Cordell Redfin
(shallow runner)

MINNOWBAITS

These long, slim plugs have a very realistic look and action. The lip is smaller and usually narrower than that of a crankbait, so the lure has a tight rocking action that more closely resembles that of a swimming baitfish.

This realism explains why many bass anglers prefer minnowbaits to crankbaits in clear water, where the fish can get a good look at the bait. Minnowbaits are not as effective as crankbaits in discolored water, because they produce much less vibration.

Minnowbaits also work better than crankbaits in cool water; they can be retrieved more slowly and still retain their action.

Like crankbaits, minnowbaits come in shallow-, medium- and deep-running models. Most minnowbaits float at rest, but some are weighted to sink and others are neutrally buoyant (below).

A floating minnowbait is usually fished with a steady, slow- to moderate-speed retrieve. Or you can alternately speed it up and slow it down. But because of its high buoyancy, a floating minnowbait is difficult to fish with a true stop-and-go retrieve, because it floats up too far and too fast on the pause.

A sinking minnowbait runs a few feet deeper than a floater and can be counted down to the desired depth to reach suspended bass.

Tips for Fishing with Minnowbaits

Use a neutrally buoyant minnowbait to tempt negative bass. Periodically stop reeling and allow the bait to "hang" right in the face of the fish.

Twitch a minnowbait on the surface to catch bass in the shallows. After twitching, pause to let the bait float back up and then twitch it again.

VIBRATING PLUGS

These thin-bodied plugs have a tighter wiggle than a crankbait and produce higher-frequency vibrations that bass can easily detect using their lateral-line sense, even in muddy water.

Because of their deep, thin body shape, vibrating plugs work especially well in waters that have similar-shaped forage, such as shad or sunfish.

Often called "lipless crankbaits," vibrating plugs do not have a lip to run interference for the hooks, so they tend to snag more easily than crankbaits.

Almost all vibrating plugs are designed to sink. Some have hollow-plastic bodies filled with shot. Not only does the shot increase the sink rate and make casting easier, it produces a rattling noise, explaining why these lures are sometimes called *rattlebaits*.

A vibrating plug will cover a wide range of depths. You can hold your rod tip high and reel rapidly so it tracks just beneath the surface, count it down to fish the middle depths or let it sink and then reel slowly to bump it along the bottom.

Recommended Tackle

A 6½- to 7-foot, medium-heavy-power baitcasting rod with a fairly light tip is a good choice for fishing vibrating plugs. It enables you to make long casts, yet the light tip prevents you from pulling the lure away too soon when a fish strikes. A high-speed baitcasting reel gives you a wide range of retrieve speeds. It should be spooled with 10- to 17-pound test mono. For maximum wiggle, attach a vibrating plug with a loop knot, split-ring or small, round-nosed snap; not a heavy snap-swivel.

Bayou Boogie (no rattles)

Cordell Super Spot (rattlebait)

The Countdown Method

4 count

6 count

8 count

10 count

Determine the most productive depth by letting the lure sink for different periods of time before starting your retrieve. In this example, the angler tried a 4 count, a 6 count and an 8 count before getting a strike on a 10 count. Repeat the same count on subsequent casts as long as you're getting strikes.

TROLLING PLUGS

Most trolling plugs have a broad forehead or long snout that gives them an extra-wide wobble but also makes them quite wind-resistant and difficult to cast.

Some trolling plugs work best at speeds of less than 2 mph while others, called *speed-trolling plugs*, have the best action at speeds of 4 mph or faster.

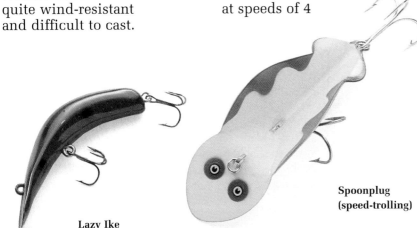

**Lazy Ike
(broad forehead)**

**Spoonplug
(speed-trolling)**

Most trollers use multiple lines and change lures frequently to determine the most productive color, size, action and depth. But when you're running different kinds of trolling plugs, make sure they are compatible, meaning that they run well at the same trolling speed.

Most trolling plugs run at depths of only 5 to 15 feet, but they can be trolled much deeper by adding sinkers or fishing with lead-core line or a 3-way-swivel rig (below).

Trolling plugs work well for fishing long, uniform weedlines or large flats. They are not a good choice for fishing humps, points or other irregular structural elements.

Recommended Tackle

A medium-heavy-power baitcasting outfit with 10- to 20-pound test superline works well for most plug-trolling situations. For lead-line trolling, select a heavy-power trolling rod and a high-capacity trolling reel spooled with 18- to 40-pound-test metered lead-core. For speed-trolling, use a stiff trolling rod no more than 5½ feet long. A lighter rod would bend too much from the strain of high-speed trolling. Attach a trolling plug with a sturdy snap or snap-swivel.

How to "Get Down"

Make a 3-way swivel rig by attaching your line to one eye of the swivel, an 18- to 24-inch dropper with a 2- to 4-ounce weight to another eye and a 6-foot leader to the remaining eye. Be sure the main line is heavier than the leader and dropper. This way, you won't lose the whole rig if you snag up.

Use metered lead-core line that changes color every 10 yards. This way, you can note the color when you start catching fish and easily return to the same color. You can also buy metered mono for precise depth control.

MAGNUM BASS PLUGS

Most of these huge plugs originated in California, where anglers were looking for big baits that resembled the rainbow trout stocked in the state's top bass lakes. These lures measure 10 to 15 inches in length, so they're used primarily for trophy-caliber bass. A good share of the plugs sold are still hand carved out of wood by local anglers and sell for $30 to $50 each.

The majority of these plugs have a sloped forehead with the attachment eye at the front. A few, however, have a crankbait-style plastic lip. A number of them have a flexible rubber tail, which gives them a realistic swimming action. Naturally, the most popular color is rainbow trout.

These plugs appeal to big bass not only because of their large size and lifelike action, they have a wide wobble that produces a low-frequency vibration similar to that given off by a good-sized baitfish.

Most anglers, retrieve or troll rapidly to generate an intense action. Like crankbaits, they work best when you interrupt their action by bumping them on the bottom or deflecting them off logs.

Some anglers have discovered that these plugs also work well when crawled slowly on the surface or "dead-sticked" over likely bass hangouts.

Recommended Tackle

Magnum bass plugs may weigh several ounces, so it takes a long, stiff rod to cast them. Many anglers prefer a 7½-foot, heavy-power, fast-action flippin' stick, but some favor a 7-foot muskie rod or a light surf-casting rod. Because a rapid retrieve may be necessary, you'll need a baitcasting reel with a gear ratio of at least 5:1. It should be spooled with 20- to 30-pound-test mono. Attach the plug with a heavy snap or snap-swivel.

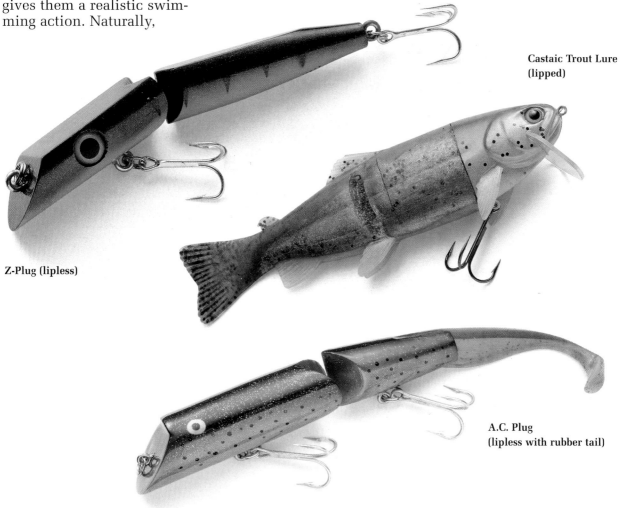

Castaic Trout Lure (lipped)

Z-Plug (lipless)

A.C. Plug (lipless with rubber tail)

LEAD-HEAD JIGS

Learning to properly fish a lead-head jig is one of the most difficult bass-fishing skills. But it's a skill you definitely need to master in order to become a complete bass angler.

Most fishermen think of jigs as lures for plying deep water. But jigs have many other applications as well. For example, you can flip them into shallow brush, yo-yo them into openings in

dense weeds or walk them down a rocky slope.

Before we get into the specifics of using each type of largemouth jig, however, you need to understand some basic jig-fishing principles:

length of the twitches and the duration of the pauses until you find the tempo that works best on a given day.

Bass tend to hit a jig on the drop, so it's important to use as light a jig as you can for the conditions. Because a light jig sinks more slowly than a heavy one, the fish have more time to react to it and you'll get more strikes.

As a rule, use a jig just heavy enough to let you maintain contact with the bottom. Windy weather or moving water requires a jig a little heavier than you would normally use.

It's important to keep a little tension on your line as the jig is sinking. Otherwise you won't feel the take. But don't keep your line too tight or the jig won't have the right action.

Fish often hit a jig with a solid thump or tap, but that's not always the case. Any twitch, hesitation or sideways movement of the line may signal a take. Or the jig may not sink the way it should because a fish has

grabbed it. Detecting these subtle takes requires good concentration.

Set the hook at the first hint of a strike. A bass flares its gills and rapidly sucks in the jig (below); if you hesitate and the fish feels anything out of the ordinary, it will immediately spit the jig.

If the water is very cold or the fish are in a neutral or negative mood, you'll have to slow down your retrieve. Inch the jig along the bottom with practically no vertical action or swim it slowly over the weedtops.

Always tie your jig directly to the line. A jig will not cause line twist so there is no need for a snap-swivel.

Bass normally "inhale" a jig as it is sinking. They flare their gills and suck in a volume of water along with the jig. The excess water is expelled through the gill openings.

JIG FISHING BASICS

Jigs are most commonly fished with a lift-and-drop retrieve. Just give the jig a short twitch (no more than a few inches long), keep your line taut as it sinks back to the bottom, and then twitch it again. Experiment with the

WEEDLESS JIGS

Fishing in dense weeds or brush is a problem with most types of jigs, because they have a hook eye that protrudes from the top and catches bits of vegetation. But a weedless jig has a cone-shaped head with the hook eye right at the front tip, so it slips through the weeds more easily. Most weedless jigs also have a bristle, wire or plastic weedguard to protect the hook point.

Perhaps the most popular style of weedless jig has a live rubber skirt and is normally tipped with a soft-plastic or pork trailer. The latter is called a jig-and-pig or jig-and-eel, depending on what kind of pork "product" you use. A trailer not only gives the jig more action, it slows the sink rate, giving the fish a little extra time to react.

Popular Types of Trailers

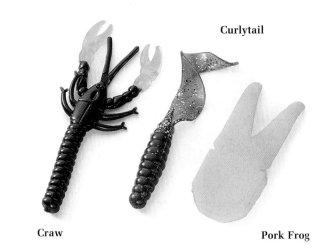

Curlytail

Craw

Pork Frog

Typical Weedless Jig with Bristle Weedguard and Live Rubber Skirt

How to Rig Popular Trailers

Rig a pork product by pushing the hook through the hole in the pork, from the bottom up.

Rig a plastic craw by threading on the narrow end as shown, letting the pincers trail.

Rig a plastic curlytail by threading it on to the start of the hook bend; the tail should ride up.

The shimmering "tentacles" of a tube jig work magic on largemouth.

TUBE JIGS

A tube jig consists of a tube head inside a hollow, soft-plastic tubebait. With the entire head inside the tube and the attachment eye poking through the plastic, the tubebait is firmly secured to the jig head. Some tube heads come with a wire weedguard so the lures can be fished in heavy cover.

Tube jigs are one of the most popular baits for sight fishing (pp. 142-143), mainly because you can give them a lot of action without moving them away from the fish. Rapidly shaking your rod tip makes the tentacles shimmer.

Most tube jigs weigh only ⅛ to ¼ ounce, so you'll probably want to use fairly light spinning gear to cast them. A 6- to 6½-foot medium-power spinning rod and a small spinning reel spooled with 6- to 8-pound-test mono is ideal.

How to Rig a Tube Jig

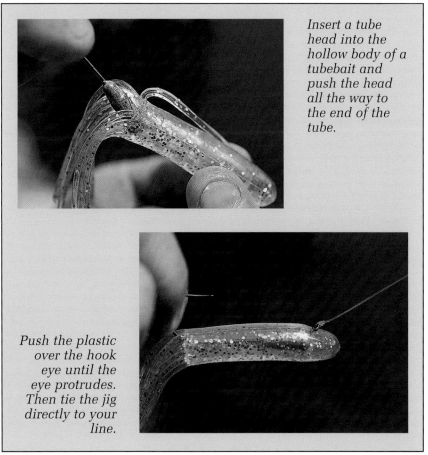

Insert a tube head into the hollow body of a tubebait and push the head all the way to the end of the tube.

Push the plastic over the hook eye until the eye protrudes. Then tie the jig directly to your line.

MUSHROOM JIGS

Mushroom jigs are used mainly for rigging with soft plastics, including lizards, craws, curlytail grubs and plastic worms. A mushroom head-plastic worm combo is called a *jig worm*.

Although mushroom jigs have exposed hooks, they are often used for fishing along a weedline or in sparse weeds. The flattened head abuts snugly with the plastic body, so there is no groove to catch algae or bits of vegetation.

The light-wire hook can be easily ripped through most weeds and, because of the double-barbed jig head, the body stays firmly affixed, even when the jig is given a sharp snap to free it (below).

How to Rig & Fish a Jig Worm

Push a plastic worm or other soft plastic onto a mushroom head jig so the body is firmly abutted against the flat surface of the jig head, with no gap.

Cast a jig worm into sparse weeds and retrieve slowly. When the open hook hangs up in the vegetation, free it with a sharp jerk of your rod.

As the bait darts upward and then flutters back down, keep your line taut and watch it closely. If you feel a tap, or if the line starts moving to the side or just doesn't sink the way it should, set the hook. Ripping the jig off of weeds in this manner usually draws more strikes than fishing it with a normal retrieve.

FOOTBALL JIGS

These jigs get their name from their football-shaped head. Because of this shape, the jig has a unique rocking action. When the head bumps into a rock, pebble, stick or any obstacle on the bottom, a pull on the line causes the body to tip up into a position that resembles a crayfish holding up its pincers in a defensive posture. When the jig passes over the obstacle, the body pivots back down to its normal position.

A football head usually weighs at least ¾ ounce, so these jigs are most often used to fish deep water. They're ideal for working deep rock piles or stair-step bluff faces.

Football jigs are often dressed with both a twin curlytail to imitate crayfish pincers, and a reversed plastic skirt to bulk up the body and mimic crayfish legs.

OTHER TYPES OF JIGS

A largemouth will strike most any kind of jig, including ordinary round-head jigs dressed with a curlytail, shadtail, paddletail or live bait.

The *fly 'n' rind* (hair jig tipped with pork rind) is most popular among smallmouth anglers in the South, but largemouth fishermen use it as well. Usually dressed with bucktail, the fly 'n' rind has an enticing "breathing" action.

For swimming over weedtops or any shallow water obstructions, it's hard to beat a slider jig, one with a horizontally flattened body. It sinks very slowly and has an attractive gliding action. Some have an upturned nose, for even more lift.

When a football jig wedges on an obstacle, the head pivots and the body tips up, creating the impression of a crayfish defending itself.

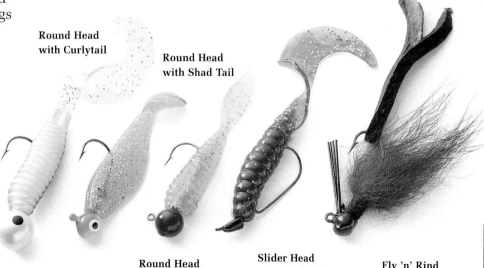

Round Head with Curlytail

Round Head with Shad Tail

Round Head with Paddletail

Slider Head with Curlytail

Fly 'n' Rind

JIGGING LURES

These heavy-bodied lures can be used in much the same manner as lead-head jigs, but they differ from jigs in that they have a built-in action.

Here are the most popular types of jigging lures and some tips for using them:

BLADEBAITS

These baits, often called *vibrating blades*, have an intense wiggle that attracts bass even in muddy water. The fish can easily sense the vibrations with their lateral line.

A bladebait has a thin, fish-shaped metal body with lead molded onto the head. The attachment eye is on the back, so the bait vibrates rapidly when you pull it upward. Most bass anglers prefer bladebaits weighing ¼ to ¾ ounce.

Some bladebaits have two or three attachment holes along the back. By clipping your snap into different holes, you can change the bait's action. With the snap attached to the front hole, the bait has a very tight wiggle; to the rear hole, a looser wobble.

Bladebaits are used mainly for vertical jigging (right). In most cases, you'll want to use smooth upward sweeps of 2

A 6½- to 7-foot, medium-heavy-power, fast-action baitcasting outfit works well for most jigging lures. For bladebaits and tailspins, spool up with 10- to 14-pound-test mono. For jigging spoons, which are often used in heavy cover, you may need mono as heavy as 30-pound test. If you'll be jigging in very deep water, consider using superline. Because it has practically no stretch, you'll get much stronger hooksets.

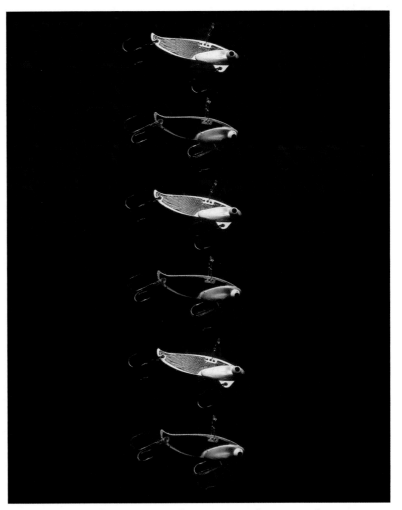

or 3 feet, but sometimes the fish prefer a sweep of only a foot or so. You can also cast a bladebait, let it sink to the bottom and fish it with a twitch-and-pause retrieve, as you would a lead-head jig. Or, you can reel it steadily, like a crankbait.

Because bladebaits sink so rapidly, they're a good choice for fishing in deep water. With a ½-ounce bait, you can easily reach a depth of 50 feet.

Bladebaits produce strong vibrations on the upward sweep; they have little or no action on the drop.

How to Vertical Jig with a Bladebait

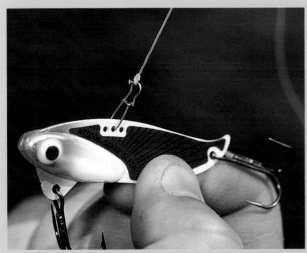

Attach a bladebait with a sturdy snap. If you use a snap-swivel, the rear hook tends to foul on the line when the lure is sinking.

Sweep your rod upward to lift the bait off bottom, then follow it down with your rod tip, keeping the line taut so you can feel a take. Use your trolling motor to follow the structure and keep your line near vertical as you drift with the wind or current.

TAILSPINS

A tailspin has a heavy lead body with a treble hook on the bottom and a spinner at the rear. Models used for largemouth weigh from ½ to 1 ounce.

Tailspins differ from other types of jigging lures in that they have good action on the lift as well as the drop. The blade spins when the lure is jigged upward and helicopters on the way down (right).

Tailspins are extremely versatile. You can make long casts and reel them steadily to cover a lot of water, work them along the bottom with a twitch-and-pause retrieve or vertically jig them.

A tailspin is also a good choice when bass are suspended. Make a long cast, count the lure down to the desired level and start reeling. Because the spinning blade provides so much lift, you can reel slowly and still keep the lure in the fish zone.

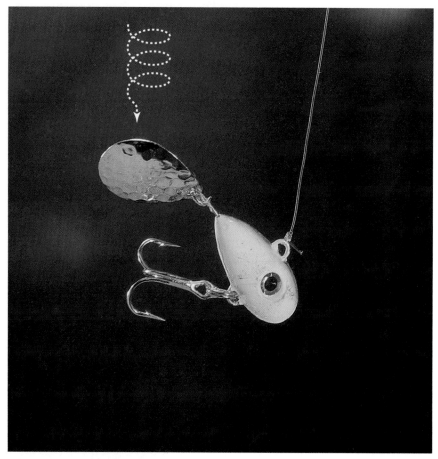

The spinning blade of a tailspin not only produces flash and vibration as the lure is sinking, it slows the rate of descent so that bass have more time to strike.

Using Tailspins for "Schoolie" Largemouth

In reservoirs with good populations of shad, large groups of 1- to 2-pound largemouth, called "schoolies," often herd baitfish to the surface in open water. Some anglers carry a spare rod rigged with a tailspin in case they encounter surface activity in open water. Tailspins are ideal for casting to schoolies because you can cast them a long distance. This way, you can keep your boat far enough away that you don't spook the fish.

JIGGING SPOONS

Made of just a piece of lead, brass or stainless steel with a hook on the end of it, a jigging spoon is one of the simplest and most inexpensive bass lures. But for jigging in deep water, it may well be the most effective lure you can buy. Jigging spoons used for largemouth usually weigh from ½ to 1½ ounces.

For vertical jigging, most anglers prefer long, thin jigging spoons because they sink more rapidly than wide, stubby ones. Work the lure just as you would a bladebait (p. 121), but use slightly shorter jigging strokes, usually from 6 to 18 inches.

There will be times when a big lift followed by a long pause works best; other times, the fish will prefer a shorter,

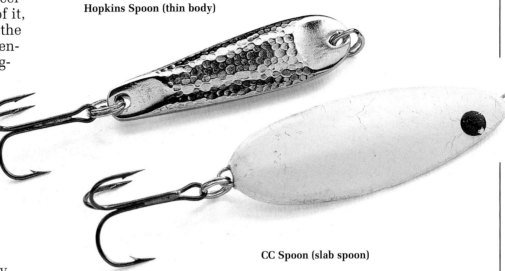

Hopkins Spoon (thin body)

CC Spoon (slab spoon)

faster jigging stroke. As with any other kind of jig or jigging lure, you must maintain contact with the spoon as it is sinking; otherwise, you won't feel the take.

Wide, stubby jigging

spoons, called *slab spoons*, are designed for distance casting. Their castability and shad-shaped body make them a good choice for catching schoolies (opposite).

Tips for Fishing with Jigging Spoons

If your jigging spoon has only a hole for attaching your line, add a split ring. If you tie on directly, the sharp metal edge could cut your line.

If you get snagged when vertically jigging in timber or other heavy cover, pull the line tight and then let the spoon drop; the heavy weight usually pulls the hook free.

WEEDLESS SPOONS

When they have to fish matted surface vegetation or dense submerged weeds, many bass pros turn to a weedless spoon because it's one of the few lures they can snake through the tangle without fouling.

Most weedless spoons have a plastic, live-rubber or feather trailer that gives them an enticing action and adds buoyancy. If your spoon doesn't have a trailer, you can add a pork strip or curlytail grub.

There are three types of weedless spoons, each of which is used a little differently:

STANDARD WEEDLESS SPOONS

The heavy wire weedguard on these metal spoons makes it possible to work them through dense, submerged vegetation. But some models have an upturned nose or lip to help them slide over matted weeds. One popular retrieve, called "grazing the grass," involves reeling just fast enough to keep the spoon above the tops of weeds a few inches beneath the surface.

SPINNER SPOONS

These spoons are similar to standard weedless spoons, but they have a spinner or propeller at the front for extra lift. As a result, you can retrieve more slowly without the spoon sinking into the weeds and fouling. The spinner also adds vibration, which helps bass locate the lure in even the thickest vegetation. These lures may be hard to find, but you can always make your own (right).

PLASTIC SPOONS

Designed to slide across the surface on their back, these lightweight spoons can be inched along slowly without sinking. Because the hook is pointing up, these lures seldom foul but, for insurance, some have bristle or plastic weedguards.

Popular Weedless Spoons

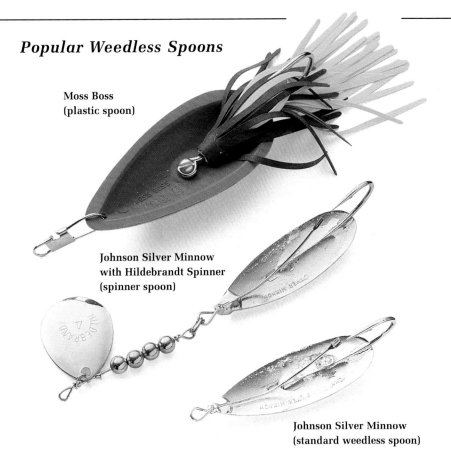

Moss Boss
(plastic spoon)

Johnson Silver Minnow
with Hildebrandt Spinner
(spinner spoon)

Johnson Silver Minnow
(standard weedless spoon)

Recommended Tackle

It takes a long, stiff rod and heavy line to horse bass from dense cover before they have a chance to tangle your line in the weeds. A 6¹/₂- to 7-foot, heavy-power baitcasting outfit and 17- to 20-pound abrasion-resistant monofilament will normally do the job. A long rod also helps keep the fish's head up, so it can't dive back into the weeds.

Tips for Fishing Weedless Spoons

Skim a plastic spoon over matted weeds using a slow, steady retrieve. This way, bass can track the lure more easily in cover where they can't clearly see it, so you'll miss fewer fish.

Keep your casts relatively short when using spoons with stiff weedguards. You'll need a strong hookset to sink the hook; if you make a long cast, there will be too much line stretch.

FLIES

When you see the water explode as a largemouth attempts to destroy your bass bug, it's easy to understand why more and more bass anglers are getting hooked on fly fishing.

But it's not just the excitement that is drawing fishermen to the sport; in the right circumstances, fly fishing is an extremely effective bass-catching method.

In years past, fly fishermen relied almost exclusively on bugs and other topwater flies for taking largemouth. That meant they were limited to fishing only in shallow water, usually around spawning time. But some innovative anglers have perfected techniques for catching bass on subsurface flies and sinking lines, so fly fishermen can now catch bass in deeper water as well.

Here are the most popular types of largemouth flies and some tips on fishing them:

TOPWATER FLIES

It's possible to catch a largemouth on practically any floating fly, even a tiny dry fly used for trout. But most anglers prefer large, bushy or noisy flies such as:

• **Poppers.** Because of their cupped or flattened face, these hard-bodied lures make a popping sound when retrieved with sharp twitches. Most poppers have hair or feather tails, rubber legs or hackle collars. You can fish a popper with a nonstop series of twitches or a twitch-and-pause retrieve (p. 129).

• **Sliders.** The bullet-shaped head makes it easy to skitter a slider over matted or floating-leaved weeds. Sliders do not create as much surface disturbance as poppers, so they may be a better choice when bass aren't in an aggressive mood.

• **Hair Bugs.** These frog or mouse imitations have a head and/or body made of clipped deer or elk hair. The hollow fibers are extremely buoyant and have a lifelike feel, so bass hold onto them a little longer than they would a hard-bodied popper. But hair bugs are more wind-resistant and difficult to cast.

• **Divers.** These flies have a clipped-deer-hair head and collar, which makes them quite buoyant. But when you strip line, they dive beneath the surface and make a gurgling noise. Bass find it hard to resist the frog-like sound and action.

Recommended Tackle

For casting topwater flies, most largemouth anglers use a 7- to 9-weight fly rod, a weight-forward or bass-bug-taper floating line and a 6- to 9-foot leader with a 0X to 4X tippet. Topwater flies in sizes 2 to 1/0 are most popular.

Diver

Slider

Hair Bug

Popper

SUBSURFACE FLIES

The most effective subsurface flies are those that have a realistic "breathing" or swimming action and closely resemble real bass food.

• **Leech Flies.** These flies have an extra-long tail, made of marabou, chamois, latex or rabbit fur. A jigging-type retrieve gives them a realistic leech-like wiggle.

• **Crayfish Flies.** With their lifelike hair or feather pincers, these flies imitate one of the largemouth's favorite foods. Crayfish imitations are normally fished with a twitch-and-pause retrieve or drifted naturally along the bottom.

• **Marabous.** The fluffy marabou wing gives these flies a seductive breathing or pulsating action when you retrieve them with short strips.

• **Muddlers.** These versatile flies have feather wings and a large head made of clipped deer hair. They come in a wide variety of patterns, some of which are intended to be fished on the surface to imitate large insects; others, in deep water to mimic baitfish.

Sinking patterns have bodies wrapped with wire. With a sinking line and a slow stripping retrieve, they can be fished as deep as 15 feet.

When retrieved with sharp twitches, a leech fly undulates wildly.

Recommended Tackle

For fishing subsurface flies in shallow water, you can use the same tackle recommended for topwater flies. But to reach depths of 5 feet or more, you'll need a sink-tip or sinking line along with a 4- to 5-foot, 12-pound-test mono leader (untapered). Most bass anglers use subsurface flies in sizes 2 to 1/0.

Crayfish Fly

Muddler

Marabou

Leech Fly

How to Retrieve Bass Flies

Point your rod directly at the fly and strip rapidly to make it dive beneath the surface. Because the deer hair traps air, the fly emits a large bubble and makes a gurgling sound. Keep your rod pointed at the fly as you pause to let it float back up. Continue stripping and pausing, varying the length of the strip and the duration of the pause to find the tempo that works best.

How to Retrieve a Popper

Point your rod directly at the fly and retrieve with a series of short strips with practically no hesitation. Or, pause after each strip to let the ripples subside before stripping again.

The Hand-Twist Retrieve

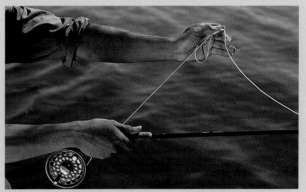

Hold the line with the thumb and index finger of your line hand and bend your wrist upward until the line catches the first joint of your little finger (left). Then bend your wrist downward so a loop of line forms in your hand (right). Repeat the procedure to steadily retrieve your fly. When using streamers or sliders, a steady retrieve may outproduce a stop-and-go stripping retrieve.

LIVE BAIT

When the bite is off, veteran anglers know that they can interest even the most finicky largemouth by using live bait.

Live-bait fishing is not only a good way to catch bass under adverse conditions, it is arguably the best method for putting a real trophy in your boat.

Here are the most popular types of largemouth baits along with some recommendations for rigging and fishing them:

FROGS

Considering the number of artificial lures that resemble frogs, the effectiveness of the real thing should come as no surprise.

Any kind of small to medium-size frog will catch largemouth, but the leopard frog is most widely used. Even so, you may have trouble finding them in bait shops, so you should know how to

The leopard frog is by far the most popular frog used as bass bait.

catch your own (below).

Most bass anglers prefer frogs from 3 to 4 inches long. How you rig them depends on the cover. For fishing shallow weeds, simply push a weedless hook through the lips. For deeper, clean-bottomed areas, use an open hook and add split-shot to your line. When fishing in

lily pads or other dense cover, be sure to use heavy line, at least 20-pound test.

Keep your frogs cool and carry them in a container with plenty of air holes. A wire-mesh box with a slitted rubber lid is ideal; it lets you put frogs in and take them out without losing any.

Tips for Fishing with Frogs

Walk along the marshy shore of a creek and nab frogs with a dip net or, if you're quick, catch them by hand.

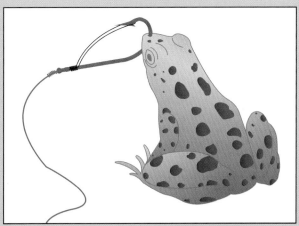

For fishing in weedy cover, push a size 2 to 4 weedless hook through the frog's lips, as shown.

Waterdogs have external gills, tiny legs and a long, unbroken fin around the tail.

Spring lizards, like all adult salamanders, have fully developed legs, no gills and a tail with no fin.

SALAMANDERS

Bass anglers use a variety of salamanders in both larval and adult forms. The most widely used type is the *waterdog*, which is the larval stage of the tiger salamander. Although some anglers use adult tiger salamanders, waterdogs usually work much better. They are available in bait shops throughout most of the country, although the supply is often sporadic. You may be able to seine your own in small ponds that dry up in summer.

Because waterdogs have gills, they must be kept in water, preferably in a styrofoam container that will "breathe." Keep the water cool (about 50°F) and change it frequently.

If you stop at a bait shop in the Southeast, you're likely to find "spring lizards," which include any of several species of salamanders found along cold springs and brooks or in cool, moist wooded areas in the eastern U.S. Although spring lizards are most commonly used for smallmouth

and spotted bass, they also make good largemouth bait.

To keep spring lizards alive, refrigerate them in an ice cream bucket along with some moist leaves or moss and perforate the lid.

Most largemouth fishermen prefer 4- to 6-inch salamanders, although some trophy specialists use waterdogs up to 10 inches long. Small waterdogs and spring lizards are often used to tip a jig. Larger ones can be fished on a split-shot or slip-sinker rig.

How to Hook Salamanders

Hook a salamander through the lips on a size 2 or 4 bait hook. If desired, secure the hook with a small plastic disc punched from a coffee can lid. Or hook it on a weedless hook, as you would a frog (p. 131).

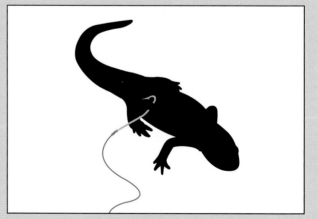

Push a size 2 or 4 bait hook through the tough skin ahead of a salamander's hind leg.

CRAYFISH

Trophy hunters who ply southern California lakes will attest to the effectiveness of crayfish as bait for the huge but extra-fussy largemouth that inhabit these clear waters. Although crayfish are commonly regarded as excellent bait for smallmouth, they work nearly as well for largemouth.

The main consideration in selecting crayfish is size. Most bass anglers prefer 3- to 4-inchers; with larger ones, you'll miss too many fish. The exact species of crayfish doesn't really matter.

Although crayfish are available in many bait shops, their sale has been banned in a few states in order to stop the spread of harmful, non-native crayfish species. You can easily catch your own crayfish by turning over large, flat rocks in a shallow stream and dip netting them as they attempt to scoot away.

To keep crayfish alive, put them in a stryrofoam container on a layer of damp weeds

Hook a crayfish by pushing a size 4 or 6 bait hook through the bony "horn" on the head. This way, the crayfish is not likely to scoot backward, crawl under a rock and get you snagged.

or moss. Keep them cool.

One of the best ways to present a crayfish is to inch it along the bottom using a light spinning outfit and 6- to 8-pound mono. But instead of reeling, use a hand-twist retrieve (p. 129). Not only does the hand-twist method give you maximum sensitivity, it forces you to move the bait very slowly to entice finicky bass.

Tips for Fishing with Crayfish

When the bass are fussy, use softshell crayfish (those that have recently molted) instead of hardshells. Squeeze the craw across the back; if the shell feels pliable, it's a softshell.

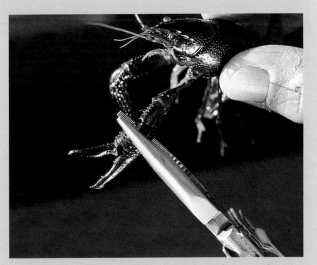

Remove the pincers of large crayfish to make it look smaller and less formidable. Just squeeze the claw firmly and it will neatly detach from the body without injuring the crayfish.

133

GOLDEN SHINERS

For decades, big golden shiners have been Florida's top producer of giant largemouths. But shiners are effective in any waters inhabited by trophy-caliber bass, including California's premier largemouth lakes.

You can buy golden shiners in bait shops throughout the country but, in most cases, these shiners are too small to interest a real trophy bass. Serious trophy hunters prefer shiners 8 to 12 inches long.

Even if they could buy shiners this size, many trophy hounds insist on catching their own wild shiners. The wild ones have a natural fear of bass; when one approaches, the hooked baitfish makes a frantic attempt to escape, a reaction that a bass is not likely to ignore. A pond-reared shiner is much less effective; because it has no innate fear of the bass, it makes little attempt to escape.

If you know of a lake with big golden shiners, you can catch them by chumming a shallow, weedy area with oatmeal. When you see the shiners dimpling the surface, throw a cast net over the school. Or try fishing for them using a tiny piece of dampened bread molded onto a size 12 hook.

Compared to most other kinds of bass bait, shiners are difficult to keep alive. It's important to keep them cool and well-aerated and to avoid overcrowding. They're especially fragile in warm weather, so they're seldom used in the summer months.

For fishing shiners in heavy vegetation, you'll need sturdy tackle and heavy line. In Florida, most shiner fishermen use a 7½- to 8½-foot, heavy-power baitcasting rod and 30- to 40-pound line to horse the fish out of the dense cover. Shiners aren't always fished in heavy cover, however. On a relatively clean bottom, a 6-foot, medium-heavy-power spinning rod with 8- or 10-pound mono will do the job.

Float-Fishing with Golden Shiners

1 *Peg a float onto your line and then hook a golden shiner through the lips using a size 2/0 to 4/0 weedless hook.*

2 *Lob-cast the shiner into a pocket in bulrushes or other emergent weeds. Don't cast into the thick weeds because the shiner will tangle your line around the stems.*

3 *Watch your rig closely; when the float starts dancing wildly or the shiner breaks the surface, get ready for a strike.*

4 *When the float disappears, point your rod at the fish, reel up slack and set the hook hard. Try to pull the fish out of the weeds before it can hang you up.*

Freelining Golden Shiners in Matted Weeds

Hook the shiner just above the anal fin using a size 2/0 to 4/0 weedless hook.

Drop the shiner into an opening in matted weeds and feed line as it swims along. After fishing one opening for a few minutes, pull up and move to another.

BEYOND THE BASICS

*N*ow that you're familiar with all the popular lures, baits and presentations, you must learn how to apply them in the real world of bass fishing.

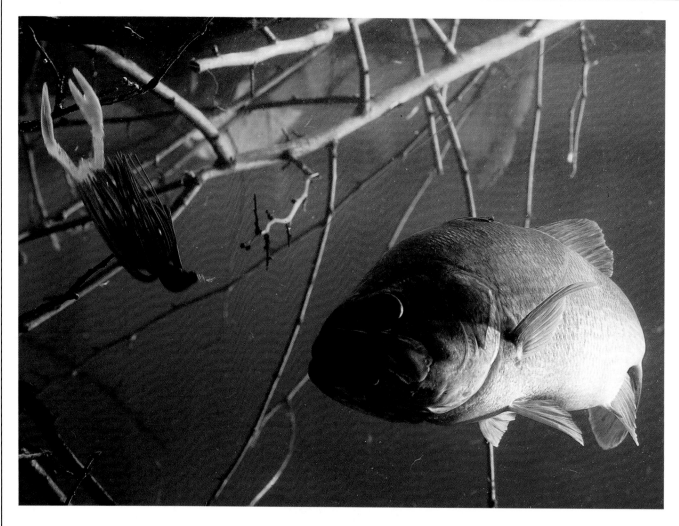

FISHING IN WEEDY & WOODY COVER

From the moment they hatch, largemouth bass use some type of weedy or woody cover. Not only does it protect them from attacks by predatory birds and fish, it affords them shade and in some cases, cooler temperatures. It also provides an ambush point where adult bass can lurk unnoticed before darting out to grab unsuspecting prey.

Weeds are the most common type of cover in natural lakes, where stable water levels allow the plants to take root. Weedy cover can also be found in slow-moving rivers, river backwaters and impoundments where water levels do not undergo dramatic fluctuations.

Woody cover is most common in reservoirs, especially in those where the timber was not cleared before the lake was filled. There, bass find ample hiding spots in the form of standing timber, stump fields, fallen trees and flooded brush. But fallen trees and brush piles are also abundant in natural lakes and rivers.

To become a successful bass angler, you must learn to contend with all forms of weedy and woody cover. Not only must you place your lure or bait in the midst of the tangle and work it effectively, you must be able to extract the fish before they can wrap your line around the stems or branches.

On the pages that follow are some important techniques for fishing in dense weedy and woody cover.

FLIPPIN'

Fishing a tiny opening in the brush or a tight pocket in the weeds obviously requires precision casting. But catching bass in this situation requires more than just accuracy: Your lure must alight very softly, with little surface disturbance, or you'll spook the fish.

When fishing nearby targets, you can place your lure precisely while barely making a ripple by flippin'. You control the line with your hand, so your reel never turns.

The Flippin' Technique

1 *Pull out as much line as you think you'll need to reach your target. Let about a rod's length dangle from the rod tip and hold the excess in your other hand, as shown.*

2 *With your rod pointed upward and in the direction of your target, swing the lure toward your body.*

3 *Swing the lure toward your target with a smooth, level motion of the rod tip. Be sure to keep the trajectory as low as possible. Otherwise, the lure will splash down too hard.*

4 *Jig the lure slowly through the cover, or allow it to catch on a branch and jig it in place. After thoroughly working the spot, pull up the lure and flip it into the next opening.*

PITCHIN'

Like flippin', pitchin' is a method for placing your lure in a tight spot so it lands softly and doesn't spook the fish. The two techniques differ, however, in that pitchin' is usually done to reach more distant targets, meaning that you're actually casting with your reel, rather than swinging line you've stripped off the reel by hand.

Flippin' and pitchin' both require a lot of practice to develop the accuracy, low trajectory and soft entry necessary for success. Before going out on the water, work on these techniques in your backyard. Practice dropping your lure into a coffee cup placed several feet back from a horizontal tree limb no more than a foot off the ground.

Recommended Tackle and Lures

The ideal pitchin' outfit consists of a 6½- to 7-foot, medium-heavy-power, fast-action baitcasting rod and a narrow-spool baitcasting reel filled with 14- to 20-pound mono. With a narrow-spool reel, the spool has very little momentum, meaning fewer backlashes. The most popular lures for pitchin' include weedless jigs and Texas-rigged soft plastics.

The Pitchin' Technique

1 Strip off enough line so that you can cradle the lure in the palm of your hand; the head of the lure should be pointing in the direction you want to cast.

2 With your reel in free-spool and the spool tension loose, hold your reel at chest level and point your rod tip slightly downward.

3 Sweep the rod forward and slightly upward to pull the lure out of your hand, and propel it toward your target on a low trajectory. Raising the rod too high elevates the trajectory. Thumb the reel to stop the lure so it settles down softly in the precise spot. With the spool tension so loose, the spool will keep turning if you don't thumb it.

Yo-Yoing

A mat of dense weeds or a thick brush pile are heaven to largemouth bass, but they're a nightmare for anglers trying to get their lure down to the fish. It would be impossible to cast and retrieve in cover this thick, but you can "yo-yo" your lure into openings in the cover.

The key to successful yo-yoing is to keep your line almost perfectly vertical. If your boat is drifting too fast, your line will trail at an angle, causing hang-ups, preventing your lure from reaching the bottom and making it far more difficult to feel strikes.

Recommended Tackle and Lures

For yo-yoing, you'll need a 6½- to 7-foot, medium-heavy-power, fast-action baitcasting rod with an extra-long handle for extra hoisting leverage. Pair it with a high-speed baitcasting reel (gear ratio of at least 6:1) spooled with 20- to 30-pound-test mono. Most anglers prefer heavy weedless jigs and Texas-rigged soft plastics (from ⅝ to 1 ounce) so they can get down quickly and keep their line vertical.

The Yo-Yoing Technique

1 Using an electric trolling motor to hold your position, drop your lure into an opening no more than a rod's length from the boat.

2 After the lure reaches bottom, jig it in place for a few seconds; if you don't get a strike, reel up and drop it into the next opening.

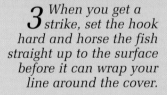

3 When you get a strike, set the hook hard and horse the fish straight up to the surface before it can wrap your line around the cover.

FISHING IN CLEAR WATER

Largemouth bass are notoriously difficult to catch in clear water; they're easily spooked by your movement or shadow, and they're quick to spot any flaw in your presentation.

Adding to the challenge is the fact that clearwater bass often inhabit a wide depth range. Because clear water is usually low in nutrients, it normally has an ample supply of dissolved oxygen in the depths, meaning that bass can go pretty much wherever they want to escape sunlight and find food.

In some clear canyon reservoirs, for instance, largemouth have been found in water more than 100 feet deep. If the fish can find enough cover in the shallows to provide shade, however, there may be no need to go deep.

If you've ever tried fishing bass in a clearwater lake on a calm, sunny day, you know how difficult it can be. Your odds are much better in overcast weather, early or late in the day or at night. Not only are the bass feeding more aggressively then, they're less likely to see you.

But some anglers love to fish clearwater bass in calm, sunny weather, because these conditions offer a unique opportunity: While the bass can see you, you can see them as well, so you can sight-fish for them.

On the pages that follow, we'll explore sight-fishing and other techniques commonly used for clearwater bass.

SIGHT-FISHING

Most anglers assume that sight-fishing can only be done in spring, when bass move into the shallows to spawn. While that certainly is a good time to sight-fish, it's not the only time. It's possible to find some bass in the shallows beginning after the first few warm days in spring until the water temperature drops below the 50-degree mark in fall.

Sight-fishing works best on calm, clear days, particularly when the sun is directly overhead. When the sun is low, it's hard to see into the water because of the reflections. Unless the water is superclear, you'll seldom be able to sight-fish at depths of more than 5 feet.

To maximize your chances

of spotting fish, wear polarized sunglasses and keep the sun at your back as much as possible to minimize glare. If there is even a slight breeze, stay along a protected bank where the water is perfectly calm.

When you can see the fish, they can probably see you as well, so be sure to wear drab clothing, keep a low profile and avoid making any unnecessary noise.

How to Sight-Fish

1 Stand in the bow and use your trolling motor to move slowly but steadily. Keep the sun at your back so you can see into the water and spot fish or any movements or shadows that indicate fish.

2 Blind-cast with a floating minnowbait, in-line spinner or chugger until you spot a bass. Then switch to a slower bait such as a tubebait or plastic worm.

3 Cast the tubebait or worm well past the fish and retrieve it very slowly. Try to make it pass at least 3 feet in front of the bass. If you get the lure too close to the fish, you may spook it.

4 If the bass shows some interest but doesn't strike, shake the rod tip rapidly to make the lure jiggle. When the jiggling stops, the fish will often strike.

SPLIT-SHOTTING

As a rule, largemouth bass in clear water are much fussier than their murky-water cousins. They inspect your offering more closely, so your presentation must be nearly flawless.

To tempt these finicky fish, anglers who spend a lot of time on clearwater lakes use a technique called "split-shotting." It involves using small, natural-looking, lightly weighted lures and excruciatingly slow retrieves.

Like sight-fishing, the technique requires spinning tackle and light line but, in most cases, you are working likely structure and cover rather than attempting to catch visible bass.

Popular Split-Shotting Lures

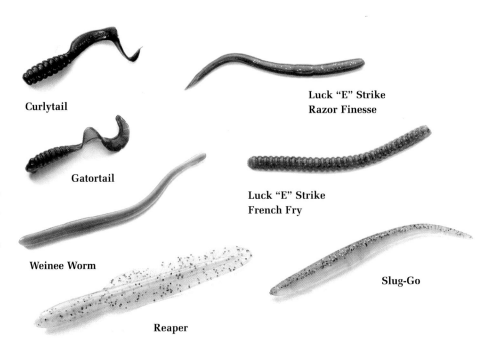

Curlytail

Gatortail

Weinee Worm

Reaper

Luck "E" Strike Razor Finesse

Luck "E" Strike French Fry

Slug-Go

The Split-Shotting Technique

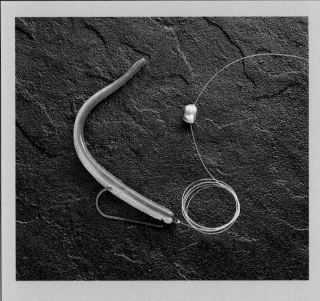

Make a split-shotting rig by pinching a split shot onto your line about 15 to 24 inches above a size 1 or 2 light-wire worm hook. Use only a single split shot heavy enough to reach bottom, and avoid the type with wings or "ears" that could catch weed fragments. Texas-rig the lure for fishing on a snaggy bottom or rig it with an exposed hook for working a clean bottom.

Lob-cast the rig using a sidearm motion (to avoid tangling), wait until it sinks to the bottom and then begin retrieving very slowly. Give the lure an occasional twitch; because it is weighted so lightly, it will lift up and then settle back down very slowly, giving the fish plenty of time to examine the lure before they strike.

Tips for Fishing in Clear Water

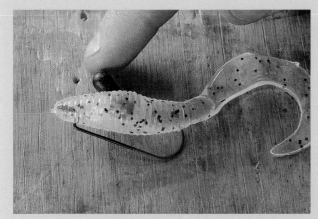

When split-shotting on a weedy bottom, cut a slit in your lure and insert a small styrofoam float (or part of one). This way, the lure will stay above the weedtops, where bass can see it.

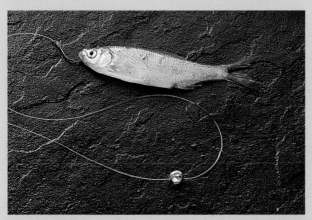

When the fish are ignoring artificials, try a crayfish, shiner or some other kind of live bait. Rig it on a split-shot rig and retrieve it very slowly, just as you would a small soft plastic.

Make longer-than-normal casts when there is a chance the fish could see you. Keep the wind at your back to make it easier to cast lightly-weighted lures.

Avoid casting your shadow ahead of the boat (as this angler is doing) when sight-fishing. Otherwise, the fish will be gone before you have a chance to spot them.

A spinnerbait is an excellent choice in muddy water because bass can easily home in on the blade's intense vibrations.

FISHING IN MUDDY WATER

In largemouth fishing, "muddy water" is a relative term. What's muddy to one bass may be relatively clear to another.

Bass that live in water that is always muddy or otherwise discolored learn to adapt to the conditions. They rely more heavily on their lateral-line sense, so they can feed with no problem even in water that looks more like heavily creamed coffee.

It's a different story, however, for bass that live in clear water that is suddenly muddied by runoff from a heavy rain. Feeding activity stops abruptly and may not pick up again until the water begins to clear.

This difference in behavior has important consequences for the angler. In water that is permanently discolored, bass are usually much more catchable. But you'll probably have to use noisy lures or those that produce plenty of vibration.

In waters that are temporarily discolored, there's a good chance the fish won't bite regardless of what lure you use. The only solution may be to find a spot where the water is not quite as muddy as in the main lake or river. It could be an isolated cove, a backwater lake or the mouth of a clear inlet stream.

As a rule, bright or fluorescent colors work best in very muddy water. Flashy lures are sometimes a good choice in waters where the visibility is a little greater.

Although catching bass in muddy water is a challenge, one thing works in the angler's favor. Because of the low clarity, the fish are not linked as tightly to cover. You can find them cruising about at random, so your casting need not be as precise.

Tips for Catching Muddy-Water Bass

Add a rattle to your lure to attract muddy water bass. Several types are available; this one fits into a slit cut into a plastic worm, lizard, craw or grub.

Use an extra-wide curlytail for fishing in discolored water. Because a wide tail moves more water, it produces stronger vibrations than a narrow one.

Add a few strands of tinsel to the skirt of your spinnerbait for extra flash. Just remove the skirt, slip the tinsel under the O-ring and then replace the skirt.

Replace the blade of your spinnerbait with a larger size Colorado blade. Not only does a big Colorado blade produce stronger vibrations, it provides extra lift so you can retrieve more slowly.

COLD-FRONT TACTICS

Nobody really knows why bass quit biting following the passage of a cold front, but there's no doubt that they do.

Black-bottomed clouds often signal the arrival of the front and the beginning of the slowdown. As a rule, things

get even worse after the front passes through and the skies clear. Fishing generally remains slow for a day or two

Enticing a cold-front bass to bite requires a skillful presentation.

after the clouds clear out.

But a cold front doesn't necessarily mean you can't catch bass. A few of the fish remain active; it's just a matter of finding them and coaxing them to bite.

Here are some pointers for boosting your odds:

• **Slow Down.** Cold-front bass are not likely to chase a fast-moving bait, but they may take a nip at one dangled in their face.

• **Smaller & Lighter.** Bass become extra-finicky after a cold front, so smaller lures and lighter line are normally the rule. Instead of tossing out a big rubber-legged jig with a bulky pork trailer on 20-pound mono, for example, try a small tubejig on 6- to 8-pound mono.

• **Tried & True Spots.** Stick to your very best spots under cold-front conditions. This is not the time for exploration. You may, however, have to fish deeper and tighter to the cover.

• **Don't Wait Them Out.** If a good spot doesn't produce after 20 minutes or so, move on to your next proven spot. This way, you'll increase your odds of finding the active feeders.

• **Look for Thick Weeds.** When the skies clear, the bright sunlight often drives bass into the thickest weeds available. Sometimes the weeds are deep, but they could be shallow as well.

• **Check Inside Turns.** Cold-front bass often tuck into inside turns on a breakline rather than hold on the points, as they normally do when they're feeding more aggressively.

Tips for Catching Cold-Front Bass

"Doodle" a Texas-rigged plastic worm in a thick weedbed by hopping it in place. Lift the worm a few inches off bottom, let it settle and then lift it again. After doodling for a minute or so in the same spot, reel up and drop the worm back down a few feet away. Adding brass 'n' glass (p. 95) makes the doodling technique even more effective.

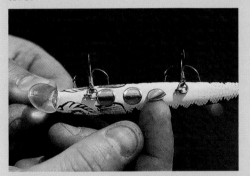

Add enough lead (such as these SuspenDots) to your minnowbait to make it neutrally buoyant. This way, it won't float up and away from the fish when you stop reeling, so they're more likely to strike than they would be if you used a floating minnowbait.

When all else fails, switch to live bait. Even the fussiest cold-front bass find it hard to resist real food, such as a lively minnow, frog or crayfish. Fish it on a split-shot rig or dangle it from a slip-bobber.

An egg-laden female may weigh several pounds more before spawning than she will after spawning has been completed.

TROPHY FISHING

The best way to catch a real trophy largemouth is to fish in waters that have a lot of them. Luckily, that's becoming a lot easier to do. With more and more Florida bass being stocked in waters outside their native range, the number of anglers who have a reasonable chance of hooking a trophy largemouth is at an all-time high.

But there's a lot more to catching a trophy bass than just fishing on a body of water that has them. If you use the same lures and presentations that work well for ordinary bass, you might luck into an occasional lunker, but it's a long shot.

Perhaps the most important thing to remember is that giant bass are basically lazy; they would rather eat one big meal than a dozen small ones, so it pays to use lures and baits that are much larger than normal (p. 153). You can also boost your odds consid-

But fishing for bass around spawning time is a topic of considerable controversy. In several states, the season is closed during the spawning period and even where it is open, many anglers have serious ethical concerns.

If you're going to fish during the spawning period, be sure to handle the bass carefully and get them back into the water as quickly as possible.

Another good time to catch a trophy is just after the females have recuperated from the rigors of spawning. Because the fish have lost 10 to 15 percent of their pre-spawn weight, they are just plain hungry. The feeding binge usually continues for 2 or 3 weeks, at which time the fish settle into their summer pattern.

In late fall, bass again start feeding heavily to provide the nutrients needed for their developing gonads. This feeding binge, though less intense than the post-spawn binge, continues until the water temperature drops into the low 40s.

erably by fishing at peak times and in prime locations.

PEAK TIMES

Ask a trophy specialist to name the very best time to catch a giant largemouth and the answer will probably be: "During the pre-spawn period." Not only are female bass at their maximum annual weight at this time, they're easy to find and feeding aggressively.

PRIME LOCATIONS

It's not difficult to find big bass around spawning time. Look for them in the shallow bays, creek arms, coves and backwaters that are the first to warm in spring. They'll almost always be around emergent weeds or brushy cover, usually at depths of 5 feet or less and sometimes in water only a foot deep.

By the time largemouth begin their post-spawn feeding binge, they've normally moved to their typical summertime locations. Start to check these spots early, however; the biggest bass are usually the first to spawn and they're also the first to resume feeding after the recuperation period.

During the late fall feeding spree, you'll often find big bass on steep-sloping structure. They evidently prefer structure of this type because it offers them easy access to deep water. This way, they can rest in the depths until the time is right and then quickly move up shallow to feed.

Tips for Finding Trophy Bass

During the pre-spawn period, look for trophy bass along the outer fringes of emergent weeds or submerged brush. The bigger fish prefer to spawn in slightly deeper water than do the smaller ones. Seldom will you find the biggest bass spawning far up in extremely shallow water.

Run the outer edge of a bed of bulrushes or other emergent weeds, closely watching your depth finder to locate the deepest water. Then fish the adjacent vegetation.

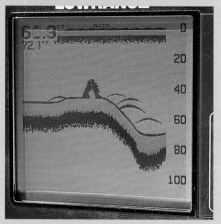

In late fall, locate bass on steep structure using your graph. The fish are often schooled very tightly, so you may have to cover a lot of water in order to find them.

Lures for Trophy Bass

Size 18 Floating
Rapala

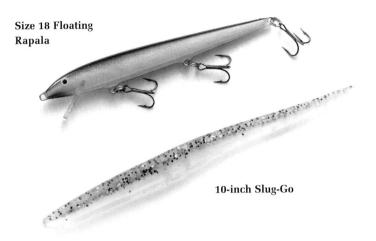

10-inch Slug-Go

Big Bait, Big Fish

Plastic worms up to 16 inches long (called snakes) are a deadly bait for trophy bass. When you first rig up with one of these huge worms, you'll feel funny ... until a big, old hog takes a liking to it!

Football-Head Jig

Tandem
Spinnerbait

12-inch A.C. Plug

Tips for Catching Trophy Bass

To find spawning bass, motor slowly through the shallows with one person running the boat and another standing in the bow, peering into the water with polarized sunglasses. When you spot a big bass, you may spook it off the bed, but you can toss out a small marker and return later.

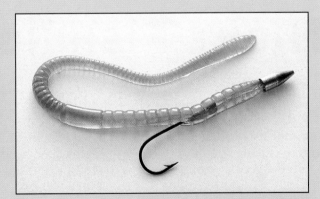

Rig an oversized plastic worm by (1) pushing the entire length of the hook into the worm and then (2) bringing the hook out the side and reinserting the point as shown. With the hook point farther back in the worm, you'll miss fewer fish.

NIGHT FISHING

There's a good reason why so many Southern anglers fish bass at night during the summer months: It's too hot to fish during the day.

Night fishing is also a good option on lakes in urban areas. Rather than deal with pleasure boats, jet skis and waterskiers, many anglers prefer to do their fishing after dark.

But social or weather-related problems are not the only reasons to night-fish. In many lakes, especially those with exceptionally clear water, bass feed more heavily at night than at any other time.

Summer is the best time for night fishing. The high sun may drive the fish into deep water or heavy cover during the day, making them difficult to find and catch. At

night, however, they cruise about and feed aggressively in the shallows.

Topwaters are the first choice of many experienced night stalkers. Bass working the shallows are not likely to ignore the commotion from a noisy surface lure.

But don't discount subsurface lures. Spinnerbaits, with their intense vibrations, work well for "calling up" bass buried in submerged weeds. Floating minnowbaits (below) are hard to beat for fancasting shallow shoals. And in some extremely clear lakes, night fishermen regularly catch largemouth on plastic worms, jigs and crankbaits at depths of 15 to 25 feet.

Other Popular Night-Fishing Techniques

Slowly retrieve a shallow-running minnowbait over shallow shoals or weedbeds where the weedtops are several feet beneath the surface. Although minnowbaits produce only minimal noise and vibration, their realism makes them very effective in clear waters.

Topwaters that make a lot of commotion with a steady retrieve work best for night fishing because bass can easily home in on them and track them. Good choices include buzzbaits, propbaits and crawlers.

Before you go out for a night of fishing, rig several rods with a variety of baits you'll be using or think you might need. Then keep the rods close at hand and ready for action. This way, you'll minimize fumbling around in the dark to re-rig or change rigs; just grab a new rod and get fishing again.

INDEX

FISHING NOTES

Fishing Notes